# The Events of January 6, 2021:
## What Impact the Second Amendment Movement?

*authored by*

Paloma A. Capanna
Attorney & Policy Analyst

**2AM Thought Leadership White Paper Series
May 2021**

*The Events of January 6, 2021: What Impact the Second Amendment Movement?* contains the facts you need to know and the questions you need to ask following the events of January 6 at the U.S. Capitol. It includes an advanced go-forward of action items for individuals and organizations to navigate current political and legal environments around "domestic terrorism," while protecting civil rights such as the Second Amendment. This publication is not intended to provide legal advice, and you should consult with an attorney concerning your individual circumstances to obtain appropriate legal advice.

Copyright ©2021 by Paloma A. Capanna

All rights reserved. No part of this book may be reproduced or transmitted in any form or by any means, electronic or mechanical, including photocopying, recording, or by any information and retrieval systems, without the written permission of the Author, except where permitted by law. Thank you for respecting the intellectual property rights of the author.

The author is not responsible for websites or website content not owned by the author.

For information about special discounts for bulk purchases, please contact the author. The author is available to speak at your live event. Please contact her, directly.

Paloma A. Capanna,
Attorney & Policy Analyst
127 Middle Lane
Beaufort, North Carolina 28516
(585) 377-7260
www.2AMPatriot.com

Photo credit: Tomas Flint, Photographer

Library of Congress Cataloging-in-Publication Data
Names: Capanna, Paloma, 1966-author
Title: The Events of January 6, 2021: What Impact the Second Amendment Movement?/Paloma Capanna

Identifiers:
LCCN:_____
ISBN 978-1-7372575-0-9 (Activist's Workbook)
ISBN 978-1-7372575-1-6 (print edition)
ISBN 978-1-7372575-2-3 (e-book)

# TABLE OF CONTENTS

|  | PAGE |
|---|---|
| **Something of a Preface** | i |
| **A Note on Methodology** | ii |

**2AM STILL AWAKE**

| | |
|---|---|
| **A – Defendants of Interest** | **1** |
|    1 – Defendants Alleged to be Oath Keepers | 3 |
|    2 – Charges Faced by These Defendants | 9 |
|    3 – The FBI's Definition of "Oath Keepers" as an Organization | 13 |
|    4 – Independent Actors with Minds All Their Own | 15 |
|    5 – Problematic Misassociations | 23 |
| **B – The Congressional Hearings** | **31** |
|    1 – The Line-Ups for the Congressional Hearings | 32 |
|    2 – The Intelligence Run-Up to January 6 | 34 |
|    3 – The Changes in Analysis on January 3 & 5 | 36 |
|    4 – Analytics on the Ground on January 6 | 39 |
|    5 – A Convenient Political Target | 40 |
|    6 – The Graham-Wray Exchange | 44 |
|    7 – The Fallacy of Equating an American Criminal to a Foreign Terrorist | 47 |
| **C – Anticipated "Domestic Terrorist" Legislation** | **49** |
|    1 – The Statutory Origin of "International Terrorism" | 50 |
|    2 – Existing Statutory Definitions of "Domestic Terrorism" | 53 |
|    3 – The FBI's Nomenclature and Analytics | 56 |
|    4 – How Does One Make the "Foreign Terrorist Organization List?" | 59 |
|    5 – Who Might Make the Initial "Domestic Terrorist List?" | 65 |
|    6 – Do Terrorism Lists Solve Anything? | 70 |
| **D – Domestic Terrorism: The New Political Whiplash** | **73** |
|    1 – "Domestic Terrorist" a/k/a "Enemy Combatant" | 75 |
|    2 – 2021: An FBI Odyssey | 79 |
|    3 – Conditions of Release | 84 |
|    4 – "Combat this Scourge" | 86 |

| | |
|---|---|
| 5 – "The Terrorism Intelligence Improvement Act of 2021" | 90 |
| 6 – "The Domestic Terrorism Prevention Act of 2021" | 91 |
| 7 – USCP: Use of Lethal Force Refresher | 92 |

**E – Call to Action: An Agenda for Second Amendment Supporters** — 93

   1 – Membership & Merchandise — 95
      E.1.a. – Membership, Customer, and Marketing Lists — 95
      E.1.b. – "Member," Defined — 97
      E.1.c. – Merchandise and Branding — 98
   2 – Candidates & Voting — 100
      E.2.a/b/c – Lobbying/Campaign/Advancing — 100
      E.2.d – GOTV – "Get Out The Vote!" — 100
   3 – Bill Watch — 102
   4 – Legal Defense Funds — 106
   5 – Go Back (To a Simpler Way of Doing Things) — 108

**Index** — 111

**Appendix 1**: Opposition Letter, S.B. 183 (Rubio)
**Appendix 2**: Opposition Letter, H.B.350/S.B.963 (Schneider/Durbin)
**Appendix 3**: Telephone Calls to Senate/House
**Appendix 4**: FBI FOIA Letter

**4 AM RISE & SHINE**

**About the Author**

*during questioning of the **FBI** Director*

"Well," said **Senator Cornyn** of Texas. "I've heard the expression that here in Washington whoever has the best narrative – *wins*. And so, sometimes, I think the narrative is created and then people try to search for facts that might bolster that narrative."

March 2, 2021
**United States Senate**
**Committee on the Judiciary**

*hearing: "oversight of the **Federal Bureau of Investigation** on the january 6$^{th}$ insurrection, domestic terrorism, and other threats"*

## SOMETHING OF A PREFACE

The events of January 6 were predictable as early as 2016, the day I sat in about the fifteenth row of the NRA presidential primary parade in the large ballroom at Nashville's convention center. I was there to cheer on Senator Cruz, the primary candidate I believed had the longest and most trustworthy history of supporting the Second Amendment. I left the convention knowing it would be Trump on the ticket.

I knew it, again, when, in 2017, President Trump nominated Neil Gorsuch to the Supreme Court of the United States. I shouted at the televised Senate confirmation hearings at the nominee's lack of knowledge or even preparation on national security, foreign detainees, and the Second Amendment. This sitcom aired reruns in 2018 and 2020.

The third strike was the first photograph I saw of the President with Enrique Tarrio, smiling, laughing, speaking encoded language designed to signal "privileged insider." "Proud Boys" was and still is: nothing. Not in active business status. Not an IRS approved 501(c)(3). Not a dues-paying membership organization. Just something tossed together by English-Canadian-lives-in-Brooklyn magazine man Gavin McInnes in 2016 for "beery meet-ups".[i] The U.S. Chapter (at least for the moment) headed by Tarrio, a man with a known history as a paid FBI informant.[ii] The Canadian Chapter declared itself d.o.a. on May 2, 2021, 90-days after it was declared a "terrorist entity" by the Canadian government.[iii]

Sadly, neither Tarrio/McInnes, nor Trump, neither Gorsuch, Kavanaugh, Barrett – none have any particular history of activity defending and upholding the Second Amendment. They are outsiders to an American civil liberty with roots older than the Constitution, itself.

And so, I do what I can do. I write this White Paper with the hope that the repercussion of the events of January 6, namely, the enactment of "domestic terrorist" legislation, is not equally as inevitable as the events of January 6.

*Paloma*

[i] Feuer, Alan, "Proud Boys Founder: How He Went from Brooklyn Hipster to Far-Right Provocateur," The New York Times (October 16, 2018), see https://www.nytimes.com/2018/10/16/nyregion/proud-boys-gavin-mcinnes.html?smid=url-share

[ii] Roston, Aram, "Exclusive: Proud Boys leader was 'prolific' informer for law enforcement," Reuters (January 27, 2021), see https://www.reuters.com/article/us-usa-proudboys-leader/exclusive-proud-boys-leader-was-prolific-informer-for-law-enforcement-idUSKBN29W1PE  See, also, Sara Sidner's interview with Tarrio for CNN at https://www.cnn.com/videos/politics/2021/02/26/proud-boys-leader-enrique-tarrio-intv-capitol-riot-government-fear-people-sidner-dnt-ac360-vpx.cnn at 7:20, *et seq.*

[iii] Yang, Jennifer, "Proud Boys Canada 'officially dissolved,' group says, after Ottawa labelled it a terrorist organization," Toronto Star (May 2, 2021) at https://www.thestar.com/news/canada/2021/05/02/proud-boys-canada-officially-dissolved-group-says-after-ottawa-labelled-it-a-terrorist-organization.html

# A NOTE ON METHODOLOGY

The "facts" of January 6, 2021 are still unfolding, even as I write this White Paper. While I could wait a year and conduct a somewhat different analysis, it's my play call to push this out. It's not so much a question of "what" happened. "It" happened. For me, it's about the look-forward while everyone else is looking backwards. The look-forward is ominous. I view my purpose in writing this White Paper as getting you to pay attention to what is, in all likelihood, upon us, in the name of "national security."

I chose EOD Sunday, April 25, 2021 as the "cut-off" for new data. The driver for this White Paper is the final section, the "Call to Action." This White Paper takes into consideration several possibilities for the upcoming months, including the potential that Stewart Rhodes, himself, could be arrested. The analytic framework and recommendations remain, regardless. There is a critical mass of information both on FBI/DOJ prosecutions, testimony, and news coverage to allow for a valid go-forward.

I used primary source materials, wherever possible. As a general statement, primary source materials are superior resources. As a modern comment, I don't trust what I read unless I drill down to the point of origin. Where I do cite media sources, I strive to cite who was first to report and I look into the "about" of each media outlet. Masses of "news" these days is nothing more than plagiarism, and badly done at that. I use media resources more often as a potential clue to keep digging.

There will be future opportunities to analyze January 6 from other vantage points. And, years from now, after the appeals are exhausted for every last defendant, a deeper analysis will join the annals of history. The question is whether the last chapter of that book will be about a "domestic terrorism" statute or its defeat?

## A – DEFENDANTS OF INTEREST

As of April 25, 2021, approximately 400 defendants have been identified for investigation, indicted, arrested, and/or charged relative to events that occurred at the U.S. Capitol on January 6, 2021.[1] Acting Capitol Police Chief Pittman estimated that in excess of 10,000 persons traversed the grounds that day, of which approximately 800 people entered the Capitol building.[2] The Federal Bureau of Investigation is clear that they are in the midst of "on-going investigations."[3] The government claims to have more than 15,000 hours of surveillance and body-camera footage, more than 1,600 electronic devices, "hundreds of searches of electronic communication providers," more than 210,000 tips, and "a combined total of over 900 search warrants."[4]

Candidly, I was surprised to find "the Oath Keepers" at the top of the media coverage on January 6 and, now, just three months later, practically a household name. It begged the questions *who are these defendants?* and *are they even members of Oath Keepers?* The obvious corollary question, at least for me: *Are the Oath Keepers being used as a convenient political target to push "domestic terrorist" legislation?*

I thus sighted-in on the defendants alleged by FBI Agents and DOJ Attorneys to be Oath Keepers. With so much chatter in the media, you would have thought many on the 6th were Oath Keepers. Not true. Initially, nine, then, ultimately, three more, for a total of twelve (12) defendants accused as members of the Oath Keepers. This dozen men and women represent 3% of those charged (400) and 1.5% of those estimated to have entered the Capitol (800).

---

[1] United States Department of Justice, Attorney's Office - District of Columbia at https://www.justice.gov/usao-dc/capitol-breach-cases.

[2] Pittman, Yogananda, Acting Chief of U.S. Capitol Police, testimony (February 25, 2021) at 1:35 on C-SPAN at https://www.c-span.org/video/?509246-1/house-legislative-branch-subcommittee-hearing-january-6-attack-us-capitol

[3] Wray, Christopher, Director, Federal Bureau of Investigation, testimony (March 2, 2021), generally, on C-SPAN at https://www.c-span.org/video/?509033-1/fbi-director-christopher-wray-testifies-january-6-capitol-attack ; see, also, Testimony, Assistant Director, Counterterrorism Division, FBI, Jill Sanborn, March 3, 2021, generally, on C-SPAN at https://www.c-span.org/video/?509313-1/senate-rules-homeland-security-committees-hearing-us-capitol-attack-day-2-part-1

[4] *U.S. v. Caldwell, et al.*, United States' Motion to Continue and to Exclude Time under the Speedy Trial Act (March 12, 2021), pp. 2-3.

I explicitly leave to others the analysis of defendants labeled "Proud Boys," "QAnon," "white supremacist," "sovereign citizen," and "anarchist." The former, the Oath Keepers, is generally not averse to Second Amendment political issues, while the latter bears zero to negative roles in the objectives of the Second Amendment Movement. It is the Second Amendment that is my number one political issue. The Second Amendment is the modern civil rights movement.

From the outset of this section, I want to emphasize that my presentation style will make it appear the government's legal documents are properly organized and structured. They are not. There is a verbose, extraneous narrative being pedaled in documents sworn to by FBI agents and attested by DOJ attorneys. The initial charging documents and indictments pull from a central, boilerplate, cut-and-paste-ready template, and yet the DOJ can't even make up their minds as to which charges to pursue.

The DOJ mindset for the January 6 prosecutions was contrived by the former Interim U.S. Attorney for D.C., Michael Sherwin, who described in an interview on March 22, 2021 for CBS 60 Minutes: "So I wanted to ensure and our office wanted to ensure that there was shock and awe that we could charge as many people as possible before the 20th [of January]."[5]

The day after the interview, DOJ launched an internal review through their Office of Professional Responsibility against Sherwin for violations of Department guidelines concerning media interaction.[6] The Hon. Amit P. Mehta, U.S. District Judge for the District of Columbia, immediately conference-called the attorneys, saying, "I was surprised – and I'm being restrained in my use of terminology – to see Mr. Sherwin sitting for an interview about a pending case in an ongoing investigation."[7]

In sum and substance? The prosecution of the so-called "Oath Keeper defendants" is as much of a circus as were the events of January 6.

---

[5] Pelley, Scott, "Inside the Prosecution of the Capitol Rioters," 60 Minutes (March 22, 2021) at
https://www.cbsnews.com/news/capitol-riot-investigation-sedition-charges-60-minutes-2021-03-21/

[6] Weiss, Debra Cassens, "Afternoon Briefs: Judge irked by '60 Minutes' interview," ABA Journal (March 24, 2021) at https://www.abajournal.com/news/article/afternoon-briefs-federal-judge-irked-by-60-minutes-interview-caesars-sues-insurers-for-pandemic-losses

[7] Barrett, Devlin and Hsu, Spencer, "Former top prosecutor in Capitol riot case faces internal review after '60 Minutes' interview," The Washington Post (March 23, 2021) at
https://www.washingtonpost.com/local/legal-issues/michael-sherwin-60-minutes-capitol-riot/2021/03/23/ebdbc992-8bf9-11eb-a730-1b4ed9656258_story.html

## 1 – Defendants Alleged to be Oath Keepers

The FBI and DOJ dubbed the alleged members of the Oath Keepers as "the stack." Want to spin a story in the press, especially out of Washington, give it a name. "The stack" was defined in the first round of pleadings as "eight to ten individuals,"[8] in tactical gear, one hand on the shoulder of the person in front of the other, snaking through the mob and entering an already-breached Capitol building. The original allegations were rapidly filed on or about January 16-18, 2021 against nine persons, who were indicted, charged, and arrested by mid-February. In mid-March, three additional men made the line-up. That made a total of twelve.

Between the charging documents and the media, it appears some of these defendants may have joined or attempted to join the Oath Keepers organization as recently as January 4, 2021, approximately two days prior. According to initial government documents, there was no direct communication with these defendants by the Oath Keepers national leadership, including, specifically, Stewart Rhodes, the founder. The first three defendants charged, according to government allegations, decided to make their own independent plans as a direct result of that lack of communication.

Here is the total list of allegations supposed to connect each defendant to the Oath Keepers. It's a handful of sentences, extracted from more than 100 pages of pleadings and indictments, as follows:

1. Thomas Edward **Caldwell**:
   - "CALDWELL is believed to have a leadership role within the Oath Keepers."[9]

     *N.B.:* This allegation was denied by Caldwell.[10] At the hearing on February 12, 2021, DOJ attorneys conceded "…the government has not found evidence that Defendant Caldwell was a dues-paying member of

---

[8] *U.S. v. Caldwell, Crowl, and Watkins*, Affidavit in Support of Amended Criminal Complaint (January 19, 2021), ¶17; see, also, *U.S. v. Watkins*, Affidavit in Support of Criminal Complaint and Arrest Warrant (January 16, 2021), ¶16.

[9] *Id.*, ¶13. The original Criminal Complaint used the softer "appears to have" at ¶15.

[10] *U.S. v. Caldwell*, Memorandum in Support of Motion for Review of Detention Order Pursuant to 18 U.S.C. §3145(b) and Motion for Release (February 8, 2021), ¶5 and ¶12.

the Oath Keepers…"[11] By end of February, Caldwell was reframed by the DOJ as an "affiliate and supporter" and "coach on the sideline."[12]

2. Jessica **Watkins**:
   - "Watkins is a member of the Oath Keepers."[13, 14]
   - "On December 29 and 30, 2020, WATKINS and BENNIE PARKER exchanged text messages in which they discussed Oath Keeper (*sic*) membership…"[15]
   - "[Watkins] said she's a member of the Oathkeepers (*sic*)…"[16]

   *N.B.*: Subsequently, at a bail hearing on February 26, 2021, Watkins stated she was "canceling [her] Oath Keeper membership."[17]

3. Donovan **Crowl**:
   - "Crowl is a member of the Ohio State Regular Militia. The Ohio State Regular Militia is a local militia organization, many of whose members form a dues-paying subset of the Oath Keepers."[18]

---

[11] *U.S. v. Caldwell*, Government's Opposition to Defendant's Motion for Reconsideration of Detention (March 8, 2021), p. 4.

[12] *U.S. v. Caldwell*, Government's Opposition to Defendant's Motion for Release (February 11, 2021), p. 4; *U.S. v. Caldwell*, Govt. Opp. Def. Mot. Recon. Detention, *supra*, p. 18.

[13] *U.S. v. Caldwell, Crowl, and Watkins*, Indictment (undated, filed January 27, 2021), ¶15. This allegation is lacking from *U.S. v. Caldwell, Crowl, Watkins, S. Parker, B. Parker, Young, Steele, K. Meggs, and C. Meggs*, First Superseding Indictment (undated, filed February 19, 2021), ¶27.

[14] *U.S. v. Caldwell, Crowl, and Watkins*, Affd. Amd. Crim. Compl., *supra*, ¶15. The original *U.S. v. Watkins* Affidavit, *supra*, ¶15 made a softer allegation that Watkins "appears to be affiliated with a group known as the Oath Keepers."

[15] *U.S. v. Caldwell, et al.*, First Superseding Indictment, *supra*, ¶41.

[16] *U.S. v. Caldwell, Crowl, and Watkins*, Affd. Amd. Crim. Compl., *supra*, ¶26; also alleged in *U.S. v. Caldwell*, Affidavit (January 17, 2021), ¶27, quoting Zuckerman, Jake, "Ohio Bartender and Her 'Militia' Drove to D.C. to Join the Capitol Breach," Ohio Capital Journal (January 13, 2021) at https://www.citybeat.com/news/blog/21147932/ohio-bartender-and-her-militia-drove-to-dc-to-join-the-capitol-breach Also found in *U.S. v. Watkins*, Affd. Support Compl., *supra*, ¶27. The author's precise language is "She said she's a member of the Oathkeepers (*sic*)…" There is no indication whether the author attempted to contact the Oath Keepers for verification of membership claimed.

[17] Cohen, Marshall, "Alleged Oath Keeper ringleader in Capitol siege ordered to stay in jail before trial," CNN (February 26, 2021), see https://www.cnn.com/2021/02/26/politics/jessica-watkins-oath-keepers-capitol-attack/index.html

[18] *U.S. v. Caldwell, Crowl, and Watkins*, Affd. Amd. Crim. Compl., *supra*, ¶14. See, also, *U.S. v. Caldwell, Crowl, and Watkins*, Indictment, *supra*, ¶14, phrased as "some" of whose members. This

- Crowl is also alleged to have given an interview to *The New Yorker* in which he "identified himself" as a member of the Oath Keepers.[19]

    *N.B.:* By late March, the government recast Crowl as a "vetted affiliate."[20] Crowl may have joined Oath Keepers after Watkins, but his membership is disputed by Watkin's boyfriend, Montana Siniff, who said Crowl "wasn't a dues paying member [of the Oath Keepers]."[21]

4. Kelly **Meggs**:
    - "On December 25, 2020, KELLY MEGGS wrote a message on Facebook that said in relevant part: "I was named State lead of Florida today."[22]

5. Connie **Meggs** – [no membership allegations].

6. Graydon **Young**:
    - "On December 3, 2020, YOUNG emailed the Florida chapter of the Oath Keepers with a membership application…"[23]

---

allegation is dropped from the subsequent government filing in *U.S. v. Caldwell, et al.,* First Superseding Indictment, *supra.*

[19] *Id.,* ¶31, citing Farrow, Ronan, "A Former Marine Stormed the Capitol as Part of a Far-Right Militia," The New Yorker (January 14, 2021); find at https://www.newyorker.com/news/news-desk/a-former-marine-stormed-the-capitol-as-part-of-a-far-right-militia The author states during the interview "…Crowl acknowledged that he was drinking…" The author's precise language is "Crowl identified himself to me as a member of both the Oath Keepers and the Ohio State Regular Militia…" There is no indication whether the author attempted to contact the Oath Keepers for verification of membership claimed.

[20] *U.S. v. Crowl,* Government's Opposition to Defendant's Motion for Reconsideration of Detention Order (March 24, 2021), p. 4, including that Watkins believed Rhodes was allowing "non-members who have been vetted" to participate on January 6.

[21] Grieve, Pete and Alfini, Michelle, "The Oath Keepers Upstairs," Spectrum News 1 (January 29, 2021) at https://spectrumnews1.com/oh/columbus/news/2021/01/28/ohio-oath-keepers-jessica-watkins-donovan-crowl-woodstock-bar

[22] *U.S. v. Caldwell, et al.,* First Superseding Indictment, *supra,* ¶36. This allegation was subsequently changed to say "state lead of Florida (presumably of the Oath Keepers)" in *U.S. v. K. Meggs,* Government's Opposition to Defendant's Renewed Request for Pretrial Release (March 23, 2021), p. 9.

[23] *U.S. v. Caldwell, et al.,* First Superseding Indictment, *supra,* ¶31.

- On December 26, 2020, YOUNG sent an email to a third-party vendor, writing, in part "Since then I have joined Oath Keepers."[24]

7. Laura **Steele**:
    - "On January 3, 2021, STEELE emailed the Florida chapter of the Oath Keepers with a membership application..."[25]
    - "The following day [January 4, 2021], STEELE sent an email to an Oath Keepers address, ..., attaching her Florida Oath Keepers membership application and vetting form..."[26]

8. Bennie Alvin **Parker**:
    - "On December 29 and 30, 2020, WATKINS and BENNIE PARKER exchanged text messages in which they discussed Oath Keeper membership..."[27]

9. Sandra Ruth **Parker** – [no membership allegation].

10. Roberto **Minuta**:
    - "...[Rhodes] said, "I'm going to designate [Minuta] as a lifetime Oath Keeper."[28]

11. Joshua **James** - [no membership allegations].

12. Kenneth **Harrelson** - [no membership allegations].

    *N.B.:* At pre-trial hearing March 15, 2021, Harrelson admitted he was a member of Oath Keepers.[29]

---

[24] *Id.*, ¶38.

[25] *Id.*, ¶52.

[26] *Ibid.*

[27] *Id.*, ¶41, see, also ¶39.

[28] *U.S. v. Minuta,* Affidavit in Support of Criminal Complaint (February 24, 2021), ¶19.

[29] Sassoon, Alessandro, "Titusville man facing federal "terrorism" charges over Capitol Riot denied bond," Florida Today (March 15, 2021) at

| | Membership Allegation Scorecard: |
|---|---|
| 1 | DOJ conceded – not a member of Oath Keepers [Caldwell] |
| 5 | DOJ – no membership allegations [C. Meggs, B Parker, S. Parker, James, Harrelson] |
| 2 | DOJ alleges submitted membership forms on 12/3 and 1/3 [Young, Steele] |
| 1 | DOJ alleges Rhodes gave membership 05/2020 [Minuta] |
| 3 | DOJ alleged no date of membership [Watkins, Crowl, K. Meggs] |
| 12 Total alleged "Oath Keeper" defendants | |

There is no substance behind the Oath Keepers accusations, as you would see in a normal prosecution where membership in an organization is of relevance to the charges. Instead, in these cases, there are <u>zero</u> allegations that any of the Defendants were involved with Oath Keepers as an organization. The legal documents do not allege the founding of Oath Keepers, the leadership structure, the local structure, the routine duties, the criteria of membership, the dues and the payment thereof, any financial or in-kind donations, attendance at meetings, participation in routine activities, demonstration of an understanding of and adherence to an ideology, and a sharing of goals. Equally, there is no allegation of involvement by any of these defendants in decision-making with established leaders. There is not a single allegation by the government that the national leadership made plans to break into the Capitol on January 6, nor is there any allegation that any corresponding duty was delegated to any one or more of the defendants.

To embellish their legally inadequate claims of membership, FBI agents and DOJ attorneys resorted to descriptions of the defendants' clothes and accessories. For example:

- "Traveling into Washington, D.C., on January 6, 2021, while wearing clothes with the Oath Keepers insignia"[30]

- "On the morning of January 6…individuals wearing Oath Keeper patches on their hats, tactical vests, and sleeves congregated in Washington, D.C."[31] Or, in another

---

https://www.floridatoday.com/story/news/2021/03/15/federal-judge-denies-bond-titusville-man-charged-over-capitol-riot-oath-keepers/4700778001/

[30] *U.S. v. Caldwell, et al.,* First Superseding Indictment, *supra,* ¶26g; see, also, *U.S. v. James,* Affidavit in Support of Criminal Complaint (March 8, 2021), ¶3.

[31] *U.S. v. James,* Affd Supp. Compl., *supra,* ¶32.

version, "On the afternoon of January 6, 2021…a troop of camouflaged-clad individuals, many of whom were also wearing combat boots, military grade helmets, and tactical vests emblazoned with Oath Keeper patches…"[32]

> "[P]rosecutors may have overstated the risk of violence because [Minuta] had worn military-style gear."
>
> U.S. Magistrate Andrew Krause
> March 8, 2021
> Ruling, bail hearing,
> Roberto Minuta

- "A close-up view of the badges on the vest of one of these individuals, seen just under the Oath Keepers emblem on his shirt, displays the Oath Keepers motto, "Not On Our Watch."[33]

- Minuta, on January 6, was "equipped with an Oath Keepers baseball cap, … a tactical vest with the Oath Keepers patch."[34]

- "…Watkins posted to Parler a photograph of herself in the same Oath Keepers uniform…"[35]

- "At the Capitol, Crowl and Watkins joined with a line of individuals wearing Oath Keepers clothing, patches, and insignia…"[36]

- "As evidenced by his attire during the Capitol riots, [Crowl] was a vetted affiliate of the Oath Keepers…"[37]

- "Behind James are a number of other individuals, believed to be Oath Keepers members or associates equipped with similar tactical Oath Keeper gear."[38]

---

[32] *U.S. v. Caldwell*, Govt. Opp. Def. Mot. Release, *supra*, p. 2.

[33] *U.S. v. Caldwell, et al.*, Affd. Amd. Crim. Compl., *supra*, ¶¶17-18 and the earlier *U.S. v. Caldwell*, Affd. Support Compl., *supra*, ¶¶16-17; *U.S. v. James*, Affd. Supp. Compl., *supra*, ¶19; *U.S. v. Watkins*, Affd. Support Compl., *supra*, ¶¶16-17.

[34] *U.S. v. Minuta*, Affd. Supp. Compl., *supra*, ¶21, ¶24, and ¶31.

[35] *Id.*, ¶22; see, also, *U.S. v. Watkins*, Affd. Support Compl., *supra*, ¶22.

[36] *U.S. v. Caldwell, Crowl, and Watkins*, Indictment, *supra*, ¶40. In the First Superseding Indictment, *supra*, ¶68, the allegation was changed to read "At the Capitol, Crowl, Watkins, Sandra Parker, Young, Steele, Kelly Meggs, and Connie Meggs joined together with others known and unknown to form a stack of individuals wearing Oath Keepers clothing, patches, insignia, and battle gear."

[37] *U.S. v. Crowl*, Govt. Opp. Def. Motion Reconsideration Detention Order, *supra*, p. 18.

[38] *U.S. v. James*, Affd. Supp. Compl., *supra*, ¶32.

These catwalk allegations are legally irrelevant to whether a defendant is a member in good standing of the Oath Keepers organization. Oath Keepers merchandise is available through its website and is not restricted to members. For that matter, clothes and trinkets can be given as gifts or found at thrift stores. Clothing worn is not an equivalent to dues paid, nor does it establish a person is taking instructions from an organizational hierarchy.

And, let's not lose sight that it is irrelevant, legally, to the charges filed, whether any of these defendants were or were not members of the Oath Keepers on January 6.

## 2 – Charges Faced by These Defendants

Numerous times since the first Criminal Complaints were filed against Caldwell, Watkins, and Crowl, the Department of Justice has changed the charges and added "Oath Keepers" defendants. The essential document flow has been (1.) Criminal Complaint with Affidavit (plus any amendments) for each, individual defendant beginning January 16, 2021; (2.) Indictment against Caldwell, Crowl, and Watkins on January 27, 2021; (3.) First Superseding Indictment adding Sandra Parker, Bennie Parker, Young, Steele, Kelly Meggs, Connie Meggs on February 19, 2021; (4.) Second Superseding Indictment on March 12, 2021 adding Harrelson; and (5.) Third Superseding Indictment on March 31, 2021 adding Minuta and James. In addition, there are various speedy trial motions, sealing and unsealing documents/discovery, and detention motions, hearings, orders, and appeals.

By April 22, 2021 documents, charges became the following:

- ~~18 U.S.C. §2 – Aiding and Abetting~~
- 18 U.S.C. §371 – Conspiracy
- ~~18 U.S.C. §372 – Conspiracy to Impede or Injure Officer~~
- 18 U.S.C. §1361 – Destruction of Government Property
- 18 U.S.C. §1362 – Destruction of Government Property and Aiding and Abetting
- 18 U.S.C. §1512(c)(1) – Tampering with Documents or Proceedings (Caldwell and Young, only)
- 18 U.S.C. §1512(c)(2) – Obstruction of an Official Proceeding
- ~~18 U.S.C. §1519 – Obstruction of Justice Destruction of Records (Young, only)~~
- 18 U.S.C. §1752(a)(1) – Restricted Building or Grounds

- ~~18 U.S.C. §2332(b)(g)(5)(B)    Destruction of Government Property~~
- ~~18 U.S.C. §2332b(g)(5)    Acts of terrorism transcending national boundaries~~
- ~~40 U.S.C. §5104(2)    Violent Entry or Disorderly Conduct~~[39]

[Charges struck through were listed in earlier documents, but were subsequently dropped from government paperwork.]

It is important that you do not get confused by the §371 "conspiracy" charge. The DOJ is <u>not</u> making an allegation that these defendants conspired ahead of January 6 *as Oath Keepers* to engage in criminal activity. This is a DOJ charge that several defendants conspired, personally, with each other, ahead of or spontaneously on, January 6.[40]

This simple list of charges illustrates that the government has ample statutes with which to charge the defendants for their alleged conduct on January 6. The charges are serious. The penalties are serious. Minimum of ten years in federal prison if convicted; possibly more than twenty years. Plus, financial penalties, upwards of $850,000.

Now let's do a basic walk-through the same list of defendants by age, home state, arrest date, and pre-trial release status. While there are countless articles across the country and around the globe covering their arrests and motions/hearings for pre-trial release, there are very few articles covering rulings that released individual defendants pending trial. Release articles tend to be limited to a single media outlet, local to the home confinement site of the defendant. You will notice these footnotes shift off national media to local media, almost exclusively.

1. Thomas Edward **Caldwell** (age 65, Virginia).[41] Arrested January 19, 2021.[42] Denied release February 12, 2021. Released March 12, 2021, with conditions.[43]

---

[39] *U.S. v. Caldwell, et al.*, US Mot. Speedy Trial, *supra*, p. 4.

[40] *U.S. v. Caldwell, Crowl, and Watkins*, Affd. Supp. Amended Crim. Compl., *supra*, ¶1.

[41] All ages and states of residence for purposes of this section are taken from *U.S. v. Caldwell, et al.*, Third Superseding Indictment, filed March 31, 2021.

[42] All arrest dates are per the DOJ website, *supra*. I also use a free, public website CourtListener.com, which pulls from the federal court PACER system. Read through the "Minute Entries" for release decisions; few were done by written order.

[43] Cohen, Marshall, "Judge releases alleged Oath Keeper and questions strength of conspiracy case," CNN (March 12, 2021) at https://www.cnn.com/2021/03/12/politics/oath-keeper-thomas-caldwell-released/index.html

2. Donovan Ray **Crowl** (age 50, Ohio). Arrested January 18, 2021. Released March 26, 2021, with conditions.[44, 45]

3. Jessica Marie **Watkins** (age 38, Ohio). Arrested January 19, 2021. Denied pre-trial release February 26, 2021.[46] Motion to renew request for release held in abeyance March 27, 2021. Remains incarcerated.

4. Kelly **Meggs** (age 52, Florida). Arrested February 19, 2021. Denied pre-trial release March 26, 2021. Remains incarcerated.

5. Connie **Meggs** (age 59, Florida, wife of Mr. Kelly Meggs). Arrested February 19, 2021. Released March 26, 2021, on personal recognizance and conditions.[47]

6. Graydon **Young** (age 54, Florida). Arrested February 15, 2021. Released April 1, 2021, with conditions.[48]

7. Laura **Steele** (age 52, North Carolina, sister of Graydon Young). Arrested February 17, 2021. Released March 24, 2021, on bond with conditions.[49]

---

[44] Hosenball, Mark, "Oath Keepers militia figure ordered held in U.S. Capitol riot, others freed," Reuters (March 26, 2021) at https://www.reuters.com/article/us-usa-capitol-security-defendants/oath-keepers-militia-figure-ordered-held-in-u-s-capitol-riot-others-freed-idUSKBN2BI367

[45] Perry, Parker, "Capitol riot: Champaign County man ordered released from jail," Dayton Daily News (March 26, 2021) at https://www.daytondailynews.com/crime/capitol-riot-champaign-county-man-ordered-released-from-jail/DVGUX3YUAVBDPNZJ3ZJN2IBPGE/

[46] Perry, Parker, "Capitol riot: Champaign County woman quits Oath Keepers, but judge keeps her in jail," Dayton Daily News (February 26, 2021) at https://www.daytondailynews.com/crime/capitol-riot-federal-judge-denies-champaign-county-woman-bond/72OKSHVPRNDPTKKD2RYHO3YPNM/

[47] Hosenball for Reuters, *supra*.

[48] Fanning, Timothy, "Capitol riot: Graydon Young of Englewood, FL released on house arrest," Sarasota Herald-Tribune (April 1, 2021).

[49] Hewlett, Michael, "Former NC officer to be released from federal custody," Record & Landmark (March 24, 2021) at https://statesville.com/news/state-and-regional/former-nc-officer-to-be-released-from-federal-custody-laura-steele-is-charged-with-conspiracy/article_e10a91df-9a3c-5587-ac40-3cca2424938d.html

8. Bennie Alvin **Parker** (age 70, Ohio). Arrested February 18, 2021. Released March 4, 2021 on personal recognizance with conditions.[50]

9. Sandra Ruth **Parker** (age 60, Ohio, wife of Mr. Bennie Parker). Arrested February 18, 2021. Released March 4, 2021 on personal recognizance with conditions.[51]

10. Roberto **Minuta** (age 36, New Jersey). Arrested March 6, 2021. Released March 8, 2021 on $150,000 bail, with conditions.[52]

11. Joshua A. **James** (age 33, Alabama). Arrested March 9, 2021. Pre-trial release denied March 12, 2021. Released April 9, 2021, with conditions.[53]

12. Kenneth **Harrelson** (age 41, Florida). Arrested March 10, 2021. Pre-trial release denied March 15, 2021.[54] Remains incarcerated.

Initially, defendants lost requests for release pending trial, appeals of those denials, and renewed requests. But there has been a shift, particularly as the shock of January 6 faded and the cases were routed to one, primary judge, who got down to the critical examination of the allegations and the questioning of prosecutors. Several defendants were released.

Watkins, Kelly Meggs, and Harrelson remain in jail, pending trial. The government has filed a request for extension of speedy trial rules. Having rushed to charge individuals as soon as they were identified, the FBI/DOJ are now in a scramble to investigate cases while they are pending. There are already disputes over pre-trial discovery materials. This could be a while.

---

[50] Marcius, Chelsia Rose, "Ohio couple among six Oath Keepers charged this week in U.S. Capitol siege," NY Daily News (February 19, 2021) at https://www.nydailynews.com/news/national/ny-capitol-riot-oath-keepers-ohio-20210219-7a5z4ahbizbcvc26auutx3j4oa-story.html

[51] *Ibid.*

[52] Lynch, Sarah and Hosenball, Mark, "Judge rules against U.S., grants bail to Oath Keeper charged in Capitol Riot," Reuters (March 8, 2021) at https://www.reuters.com/world/us/judge-rules-against-us-grants-bail-oath-keeper-charged-capitol-riot-2021-03-08/

[53] Mahan, Anna, "Marshall Co. man arrested in connection to Capitol riots to be released from prison," WAFF (April 9, 2021) at https://www.waff.com/2021/04/09/marshall-co-man-arrested-connection-capitol-riots-released-prison/

[54] Sassoon for Florida Today, *supra.*

## 3 – The FBI's Definition of "Oath Keepers" as an Organization

In legal documents, the FBI/DOJ use two, slightly different paragraphs to depict the Oath Keepers. These paragraphs have been repeated, innumerably, by media outlets since the first criminal charges were filed on January 16. Initially, this allegation:

> "The Oath Keepers are a large but loosely organized collection of militia who believe that the federal government has been co-opted by a shadowy conspiracy that is trying to strip American citizens of their rights. Though the Oath Keepers will accept anyone as members, what differentiates them from other anti-government groups is their explicit focus on recruiting current and former military, law enforcement, and first-responder personnel. The organization's name alludes to the oath sworn by members of the military and police to defend the Constitution "from all enemies, foreign and domestic." The Oath Keepers are led by PERSON ONE." [55] [*N.B.:* some later documents use Stewart Rhodes' name in place of "Person One."]

Then, the description changed somewhat to this allegation:

> "The Oath Keepers are a large but loosely organized collection of individuals, *some of whom are associated with* militias. *Some members of the Oath Keepers believe* that the federal government has been coopted by *a cabal of elites* actively trying to strip American citizens of their rights. Though the Oath Keepers will accept anyone as members, they explicitly focus on recruiting current and former military, law enforcement, and first-responder personnel. The organization's name alludes to the oath sworn by members of the military and police to defend the Constitution "from all enemies, foreign and domestic." The Oath Keepers are led by [Rhodes]. (emphasis added)"[56]

The FBI also, in their Affidavit against Watkins, refers to "an archive of the Oath Keepers website created on December 24, 2020," specifically a "mission statement." The FBI Agent remarked:

---

[55] *U.S. v. Caldwell, Crowl, and Watkins*, Indictment, *supra*, ¶12; see, also, *U.S. v. Caldwell, Crowl, and Watkins*, Affd. Support Amd. Crim. Compl., *supra*, ¶12; see, also, *U.S. v. Watkins*, Affidavit, *supra*, ¶13.

[56] *U.S. v. Caldwell, et al.*, First Superseding Indictment, *supra*, ¶11.

> "Based on this mission statement – including that Oath Keepers swear not to obey orders that they consider unconstitutional – as well as <u>additional information gained</u> in the course of my investigation, I am aware that Oath Keepers will violate federal law if they believe their cause is just. (emphasis added)"[57]

The same Agent commented:

> "Members of the Oath Keepers <u>have been arrested</u> in connection with a wide range of criminal activities, including various firearms violations, conspiracy to impede federal workers, possession of explosives, and threatening public officials. (emphasis added)"[58]

No definition of "additional information gained." No specifics provided to support the allegation of prior arrests. There are no allegations of prior convictions. Inadmissible, as drafted.

None of this *Minority Report*-styled language serves any purpose to the criminal charges.[59] The DOJ uses "Affidavits" from FBI Agents to publish this ramble, sometimes on pages so rushed out they are no more than single-spaced, first drafts. The phrases are non-specific, offering no who, what, where, when, why, or how as otherwise required by pleading rules. Deleting every allegation about the Oath Keepers would cost government attorneys nothing. It would, in fact, create tighter pleadings. It would lessen the prosecutorial burden. No legal purpose is served by DOJ attorneys including these allegations in pleadings and other pleading-stage court submissions.

This sub-par legal and intelligence work is the tell that employees at the DOJ and FBI are working under marching orders. It deflects the government's own security failures on January 6. It advances the legislative agenda. And, even if neither of those priorities is accomplished, it discredits and destabilizes the Oath Keepers as an organization.

> "So I wanted to ensure and our office wanted to ensure that there was shock and awe that we could charge as many people as possible before the 20th."
>
> Michael Sherwin
> Former Interim Attorney for D.C.
> U.S. Attorney's Office

---

[57] *U.S. v. Watkins*, Affidavit, *supra*, ¶14.

[58] *Id.*, ¶13. This allegation is absent from *U.S. v. Caldwell, Crowl, and Watkins*, Affd. Supp. Amended Compl." *supra*, refer to ¶15.

[59] Spielberg, Steven (Director). (2002). *Minority Report* [Film]. Twentieth Century Fox, Dreamworks Pictures, Cruise/Wagner Productions.

## 4 – Independent Actors with Minds All Their Own

Far from establishing a *prima facie* case that these defendants are members of the Oath Keepers, the government's documents detail that various of these defendants cooked up their own plans. To hear the FBI and the DOJ tell it, several of these men and women rejected and mocked Rhodes, personally, and as a national leader of the Oath Keepers, and simply went along their merry way.

It's worth looking in more detail at the government allegations about the first three charged as "Oath Keeper" defendants, namely Caldwell, Watkins, and Crowl.

Caldwell was the first person charged as an Oath Keeper and the first defendant the government conceded was never a member of the Oath Keepers. Caldwell denied membership in the Oath Keepers,[60] claimed employment with the FBI, claimed "Top Secret government clearance since 1979," and claimed to be a government contractor for the DOJ.[61] Among other things.

The thing about Caldwell is that when you isolate allegations about him from the messy government pages that mix-up allegations about multiple defendants in single documents, you end up not with a question whether Caldwell was an Oath Keeper. You end up with a question whether Caldwell is an old school FBI provocateur. In his own words: "I am such an instigator!"[62] and "…I am a rabble rouser of the first order…"[63]

Caldwell wanted others to think he was important, tossing around statements like: "I picked up Signal which is a free app that is encrypted talk and text. That's how I do some secure comms with the Oathkeepers (*sic*)."[64] And: "I have been on the Oathkeepers (*sic*) intel net for months now."[65] Caldwell pushes in, over and over, ingratiating himself through phrases like "I would like to meet some of the guys *if you think I'm cool enough*. (emphasis added)"[66]

---

[60] *U.S. v. Caldwell*, Memo. Support Mot. Rvw. Detention, *supra*, ¶5 and ¶12.

[61] *Id.*, ¶2, ¶55.

[62] *U.S. v. Caldwell, Crowl, and Watkins,* Affd. Support Amd. Crim. Compl., *supra*, ¶35.

[63] *U.S. v. Caldwell*, Mot./Memo. Support Reconsider. Detention (March 2, 2021), pp. 14-15.

[64] *U.S. v. Caldwell*, Gov. Opp. Mot. Reconsider Detention, *supra*, p. 5.

[65] *Id.*, Exhibit 1, p. 1.

[66] *U.S. v. Caldwell*, Govt. Opp. Def. Mot. Release, *supra*, p. 7.

Ahead of the December 2020 MAGA rally, Caldwell messaged Crowl, claiming "I know it's not my place, but I'm sure you will have seen enough to know I am already working on the next D.C. op."[67] On December 5, 2020, Caldwell texted a contact, ratcheting himself higher with "…maybe I should be planning a MUCH bigger op, for like when we have to roll into town to actually save the Republic."[68]

By December 12, 2020, Caldwell started trying to recruit others to his scheme:

> "I was thinking. Regardless of what popeye does,[69] maybe we should get, ideally, 3 four man teams with a 2 man quick reaction force and 2 drivers/exractors (*sic*) to double as snipers/stallers (I'll explain those later) and go hunting after dark for those cockroaches who prey on the weak. This could be done even after a day of protection duty downtown if a safe house was located nearby for short rest and refit. Easy. 2 x 8 man vans would be needed for dependable transport, redeploy and/or extract. Easy. Just sayin'. It could be done."[70]

On January 1-2, 2021, Caldwell sent Facebook messages to Crowl, "Stewie [Rhodes] never contacted me so <u>Sharon and I are going our way</u> (emphasis added)."[71] Also, "I don't know if Stewie has even gotten out his call to arms but it's a little friggin (*sic*) late. <u>This is one we are doing on our own</u> (emphasis added)."[72]

Caldwell's professed ideas continued to spiral, and by January 3, 2021, he texted:

> "Can't believe I just thought of this: how many people either in the militia or not (who are still supportive of our efforts to save the Republic) have a boat on a trailer that could handle a Potomac

---

[67] *U.S. v. Caldwell*, Gov. Opp. Def. Mot. Release, *supra*, p. 4.

[68] *Id.*, p. 6.

[69] Believed to be a reference to Rhodes, who wears an eye patch.

[70] *U.S. v. Caldwell*, Gov. Opp. Def. Mot. Release, *supra*, p. 5.

[71] *U.S. v. Caldwell, Crowl, and Watkins*, Affd. Supp. Amended Crim. Compl., *supra*, ¶48g; *U.S. v. Caldwell, et al.*, First Superseding Indictment, *supra*, ¶49; see, also, *U.S. v. Caldwell*, Govt. Opp. Def. Mot. Release, *supra*, p. 8. *N.B.:* Caldwell's wife, Sharon, was not charged, in spite of numerous references by Caldwell to her quoted in DOJ documents, such as "Sharon was right with me!" See, e.g., *U.S. v. Caldwell*, Affd. Supp. Amd. Crim. Compl., *supra*, ¶35. No one appears to be asking about her, nor has any explanation been otherwise offered by DOJ on point.

[72] *U.S. v. Caldwell, Crowl, and Watkins*, Affd. Supp. Amended Crim. Compl., *supra*, ¶48e; *U.S. v. Caldwell*, Affd. Compl., *supra*, ¶33; see also, *U.S. v. Caldwell, et al.*, First Superseding Indictment, *supra*, ¶51, as well as the Indictment, *supra*, ¶35; see, also, *U.S. v. Caldwell*, Govt. Opp. Defendant's Mot. Release," *supra*, p. 9.

> crossing? If we had someone standing by at a dock ramp (one near the Pentagon for sure) we could have our Quick Response Team with the heavy weapons standing by, quickly load them and ferry them across the river to our waiting arms. I'm not talking about a bass boat. Anyone who would be interested in supporting the team this way? I will buy the fuel. More or less be hanging around sipping coffee and maybe scooting on the river a bit and pretending to fish, then if it all went to shit, our guy loads our weps AND Blue Ridge Militia weps and ferries them across Dude! If we had 2 boats, we could ferry across and never drive into D.C. at all!!!! Then get picked up. Is there a way to PLEASE pass the word among folks you know and see if someone would jump in the middle of this to help. I am spreading the word, too. Genius if someone is willing and hasn't put their boat away for the winter."[73]

Caldwell's language allowed the DOJ to portray "Far from an ancillary player who became swept up in the moment, Caldwell was a key figure who put into motion the violence that overwhelmed the Capitol. And, had all of Caldwell's plans come to life, he appeared ready and willing to wreak even more havoc."[74]

Mind you, Caldwell's lawyer dished it right back, asserting "…the Government has the ability to craft indictments in an effort to craft the appearance of wrongdoing and to forum shop" and has filed charges "…as a vehicle to assist in denying his release for vindictive purposes…"[75] Caldwell's attorney told *The Washington Post* the indictment was "a deliberate attempt to find a scapegoat for activities on January 6."[76]

Let's take a minute to review Caldwell's resume claims. Start with the claim that Caldwell was a government contractor, and run through a standard list of searches that generally gives a list of results. It appears Caldwell's company may be "Progressive Technologies Management,"

---

[73] *Ibid.*

[74] *Id.*, p. 17.

[75] *U.S. v. Caldwell,* Memo. Support Mot. Rvw. Detention Order, *supra,* ¶¶23, 25. *N.B.:* "vindictive" of what is not defined in the filings, nor was the accusation denied by DOJ.

[76] Hsu, Spencer, Weiner, Rachel, and Jackman, Tom, "Self-styled militia members in three states began planning in November for recruits, weapons ahead of Capitol breach, U.S. alleges," The Washington Post (January 27, 2021) at https://www.washingtonpost.com/local/legal-issues/self-styled-militia-members-in-three-states-began-planning-in-novembe-for-recruits-weapons-ahead-of-capitol-breach-us-alleges/2021/01/27/f13b0bfc-60b9-11eb-9061-07abcc1f9229_story.html

established in 2000, basis the government contracts database.[77] The company is not registered with the State of Virginia.[78] The domain name link on the government contract website does not work. The contracts listed exceed $6.5 million with the DOJ, the Army, and the DEA from 2004-2007. A 2007 business listing for military contractors described the company product/services as:

> "Cognos software sales and implementation, customized redaction and information-sharing solutions, enterprise architecture modernization, database technical services, including database design, administration, data consolidation and information security with oracle and Microsoft technologies."[79]

The company DUNS number was last updated in 2008 and has expired.[80] A search of USASpending.gov for the contracts, the DUNS, the company, and the man yielded no results.[81] What, exactly, it is that Caldwell did for the DOJ/Army/DEA to get paid several million dollars is unknown to this analyst.

Additionally, consider Caldwell's claim that he was an FBI section chief from 2009-2010. This bold assertion about FBI employment went unanswered by the Bureau, either within the criminal suit or through the media. No one from the FBI has uttered the infamous "we can neither confirm, nor deny…" The media, itself, simply repeats Caldwell's claim, without any reporter indicating he or she has attempted to verify it.

Across a span of several weeks, working and reworking search strings, using any available data point, there's almost nothing to find about this 66-year-old man to support defense claims on any aspect of his resume. Even defense counsel's claim that Caldwell retired as a Lieutenant Commander from the Navy could not be verified through the Congressional Register.

Caldwell awaits trial at his 20-acre farm in Virginia.

---

[77] See https://www.governmentcontracts.us/government-contractors/company-BSG2411603-progressive-technologies-management-Berryville-VA.htm   The address listed matches Caldwell's residential address, per NeighborWho.com.

[78] Virginia State Corporation Commission, Clerk's Information System at https://cis.scc.virginia.gov/

[79] AFCEA International, Signal (February 2007), p. 118, at http://www.defence.org.cn/aspnet/vip-usa/UploadFiles/2008-04/SGNL_20070201_Feb_2007.pdf

[80] See DUNS 148089480 at https://cage.report/DUNS/148089480  A "DUNS" number identifies a company's Dun & Bradstreet business credit file, and is required for submission of a government contract bid.

[81] See USASpending.gov at https://www.usaspending.gov/search

Like Caldwell, Watkins, too, has gaps in her background that can't be readily answered. And, like Caldwell, Watkins has more of an individual story pertaining to January 6 than anything related to the Oath Keepers.

Watkins wanted to be in charge. In an exchange with Caldwell on December 30, 2020, Caldwell apparently complained "Have been contacted by NO ONE. Typical [Rhodes]." Watkins replied (in part) "If [Rhodes] isn't making plans, I'll take charge myself, and get the ball rolling (emphasis added)."[82]

Watkins lives with Montana Siniff above their bar, the Jolly Roger Bar & Grill, in Woodstock, Ohio.[83] They may have opened the bar in 2018, but the business is not registered with the Ohio Secretary of State.[84] They may be serving liquor, but there is no government-issued liquor license.[85] Neither Watkins nor Siniff are registered to vote, basis that address.[86]

On Sunday, January 17, 2021, the FBI served a warrant at Watkin's residence in the pre-dawn hours. Siniff woke to lights and the sound of "This is the FBI with a warrant." The FBI escorted him out,

> ### Panther 21
>
> "Detective Joseph Coffey testified that among the items taken from the apartment were miscellaneous materials of a "**revolutionary nature**." These included **posters** of Huey Newton; Mao Tse-tung, and two black athletes raising clenched fists at the Olympic games in Mexico. Asked how he felt the posters related to the arrest warrant the officers carried, Coffey said that he thought they could be used as evidence in the **conspiracy charges**. The posters were later withdrawn from evidence by the prosecution."
>
> "**Panther 21** trial opens in New York"
> by Rod Such
> for The Guardian
> February 14, **1970**

---

[82] *U.S. v. Caldwell, et al.*, First Superseding Indictment, *supra*, ¶43; see also *U.S. v. Caldwell, Crowl, and Watkins*, Indictment, *supra*, ¶28.

[83] Alfini for Spectrum News, *supra*.

[84] Ohio Secretary of State Business Search at https://businesssearch.ohiosos.gov/

[85] Ohio Division of Liquor Control at
https://www.comapps.ohio.gov/liqr/liqr_apps/PermitLookup/PermitHolderOwnership.aspx

[86] See https://voterrecords.com/

and proceeded to throw flash-bangs through the upstairs apartment window.[87]

According to Siniff (Watkins was not there at the time), the FBI took "The Anarchist Cookbook" but left the guns and the ammo.[88, 89]

Like Caldwell, Watkins presents an example of someone speaking in grandiose terms. Consider two sentences by Watkins in the same interview, January 19, with a local reporter, prior to her arrest. On the one hand, she says her "unit, known as the Ohio State Regular Militia, has patrolled a total of 12 protests in the last year in Louisville, Cleveland, Columbus and Pickerington as well as a 'MAGA Caravan' in Champaign County."[90]

Sounds impressive, right? But, in the same interview, when discussing the Columbus (Ohio Statehouse) patrol, Watkins defined the "unit" as herself, Crowl, and "one other person," saying "the three were there to protect people."[91] According to Siniff, Watkins only recruited one other person to her militia, and the person did not stick with it.[92]

Watkins' background is a series of start-stops, most recently, as of late 2018, including the "Ohio State Regular Militia." Served U.S. Army (2002-2004), including deployment to Afghanistan in an infantry unit.[93] Changed name from Jeremy David Watkins through court order in Rochester, NY (2005).[94] Worked in Delaware. Spent four years in North Carolina (2010-2014) as an EMT and fire fighter for the Stoney Point Fire Department (Fayetteville, NC). Returned to

---

[87] Grieve for Spectrum News 1, *supra*.

[88] *Ibid.*

[89] *Ibid. N.B.:* "The Anarchist Cookbook" by William Powell (1971). *N.B.:* 141 pages of the FBI's file on Powell are available at https://vault.fbi.gov/william-powell/william-powell-part-01-of-01/view Note, also, how DOJ attorneys cast this widely-available book as "recipe for making a destructive device" and "…a chilling bomb making recipe that fortunately was not." *U.S. v. Watkins,* Govt. Memo. Support Pre-Trial Detention, *supra,* pp. 13, 17.

[90] Zuckerman, Jake, "Oath Keepers' leader wanted to 'storm the capitol in Ohio,' feds say," Ohio Capital Journal (January 19, 2021) at https://ohiocapitaljournal.com/2021/01/19/oath-keepers-leader-wanted-to-storm-the-capitol-in-ohio-feds-say/

[91] *Ibid.*

[92] Garrison, Jessica and Bensinger, Ken, "Meet the Woman Facing Some of the Most Serious Capitol Riot Charges," BuzzFeedNews.com (January 26, 2021) at https://www.buzzfeednews.com/article/jessicagarrison/conspiracy-charge-ohio-militia-capitol

[93] Cohen for CNN, *supra*.

[94] *IMO Name Change Jeremy David Watkins [to] Jessica Marie Watkins,* Supreme Court, Monroe County (March 1, 2005).

Ohio; worked in a retail store. Then, the bar in 2018 and then added the militia "unit" in 2019.[95] There are gaps from 2005-2010 and 2014-2018 that could not be resolved through the Internet and public on-line records.

According to one newspaper, Watkins grew up outside Columbus.[96] If so, and having moved back to Ohio, she was not without membership options for militia and prepper groups, already established throughout the state. The Irregulars of Ohio Reserve Militia.[97] Reapers Constitutional Militia and Heartland Defenders.[98] According to one article, Ohio had seventeen groups considered to be militias in 2020.[99]

What was it that motivated Watkins to start her own "unit" and seek direct contact with the founder of the Oath Keepers, specifically, and by name, even though she had only, at best, herself and two others to offer? There is no indication she had prior involvement with an established militia or that she attempted to participate in one. It just popped up after a gap in her whereabouts.

The Jolly Roger appears now closed,[100] and Watkins remains behind bars.

---

[95] Caniglia, John, "How an Ohio bartender's patriotism was warped by social media and a devotion to Trump, ending in conspiracy charges from the Capitol riots," Cleveland.com (April 11, 2021) at https://www.cleveland.com/politics/2021/04/how-an-ohio-bartenders-patriotism-was-warped-by-social-media-and-a-devotion-to-trump-ending-in-conspiracy-charges-from-the-capitol-riots.html?outputType=amp

[96] *Ibid.*

[97] Albrecht, Brian, "Ohio's militias are armed and ready, with good intent they say" Cleveland.com (July 28, 2019) at https://www.cleveland.com/news/g66l-2019/07/b4f96332c38390/ohios-militias-are-armed-and-ready-with-good-intent-they-say.html

[98] Albrecht, Brian, "What do Ohio militia members say about the Capitol attack?" Cleveland.com (February 21, 2021) at https://www.cleveland.com/news/2021/02/what-do-ohio-militia-members-say-about-the-capitol-attack.html

[99] Mitchell, Madeline, "Likely to grow even worse.' Ohio ranks No. 2 for most extremist anti-government groups," Cincinnati.com (February 8, 2021, part of Gannett/USA Today Network) at https://www.cincinnati.com/story/news/2021/02/08/ohio-ranks-no-2-most-extremist-anti-government-groups/4438357001/

[100] Amari, Farnoush and Sewell, Dan, "Ohio town unknowingly hosted alleged Capitol attack plotters," The Cincinnati Enquirer (January 29, 2021) at https://www.cincinnati.com/story/news/2021/01/29/ohio-town-unknowingly-hosted-alleged-capitol-attack-plotters/4306131001/

Crowl has multiple priors, and he's already out on bail. Crowl confirmed in an interview with *The New Yorker*: DUI arrest in 2020, violation of probation, and domestic violence.[101] Crowl said he was drinking alcohol during that interview, and the article quotes a friend as saying Crowl has struggled with addiction.[102] Another individual described Crowl is "recognizable as a loud figure who is at the bar just about every night."[103] A review of on-line public records includes tax liens and foreclosure actions, against him, as well.[104]

At a glance, Crowl has little legal value. It would be difficult to establish Crowl as a credible witness, one way or the other, concerning membership, motivation, and recall.

But, here's the problem with being too quick to discount Crowl: a Facebook message from Crowl to a non-defendant third-party may be the best description of the anticipated agenda for January 6. As alleged by the government: January 6, 2021 at 3:08 am Crowl wrote "We are doing the W.H. in the am and early afternoon, rest up at the Hotel, then headed back out tomorrow night "tifa" hunt'in (*sic*)."[105] Assuming "W.H." means White House, what DOJ attorneys call "inside knowledge" of the "covert" Oath Keeper operations[106] would appear to defeat DOJ arguments that the defendants had any intention, prior to January 6, to be at the Capitol building. The hundreds of pages of legal documents otherwise give almost no attention to where anyone intended to be or was on January 6 prior to arriving at the Capitol building.

The analytic struggle of the government forcing the narrative of these individuals onto the Oath Keepers organization is that none of these defendants are claimed to have invested time or money into the organization. And, there is every indication of at least a few defendants functioning as independent, if not rogue, actors. If not on behalf of the FBI.

---

[101] The New Yorker, *supra*.

[102] *Ibid*.

[103] Alfini for Spectrum News, *supra*.

[104] Champaign County Ohio on-line records search at
https://eservices.champaignclerk.com/eservices/searchresults.page

[105] *U.S. v. Crowl*, Govt Opp. to Def. Mot. Reconsideration Detention Order, *supra*, p. 7.

[106] *Ibid*.

## 5 – Problematic Misassociations

On April 16, 2021, just as I thought I was in the home stretch of defendant research and analysis, having put up for weeks with the single messiest DOJ prosecutions I have ever tracked, the United States Department of Justice committed its worst injustice to date in this matter. It pushed out an official "Press Release" from its Office of Public Affairs titled "Lifetime Founding Member of the Oath Keepers Pleads Guilty to Breaching Capitol on Jan. 6 to Obstruct Congressional Proceeding."[107] The DOJ PR had its intended effect: immediate headlines, radio and TV broadcasts, and social media noise. There is not enough white space in a ream of paper to capture the feeding frenzy this PR caused. The melodrama of the PR included: "On this 100th day since the horrific January 6 assault on the United States Capitol..."[108]

The previous week, the headlines were that the same defendant was cooperating with the DOJ concerning the Proud Boys,[109] a different group.

The subject of the DOJ big tent attraction is Jon Schaffer. Schaffer, age 53, of Indiana, is a founding member of "Iced Earth," a heavy metal band. Media outlets like *Variety* wrote about his arrest, pointing out his "notoriety in the metal community and an unusually long, white goatee got him singled out quickly."[110] According to *Variety*, Iced Earth has released twelve, original studio albums since 1990, most recently in 2017 – "Incorruptible" – the group's "chart peak to date".[111] Schaffer produced the album and wrote or co-wrote the songs.[112]

---

[107] U.S. Department of Justice, Office of Public Affairs (April 16, 2021) at https://www.justice.gov/opa/pr/lifetime-founding-member-oath-keepers-pleads-guilty-breaching-capitol-jan-6-obstruct ; see also *U.S. v. Schaffer,* Information (April 16, 2021).

[108] *Ibid.*

[109] Polantz, Katelyn, "Capitol riot defendant flips to help prosecutors against Proud Boys," CNN (April 7, 2021) at https://www.cnn.com/2021/04/07/politics/capitol-riot-flip-proud-boys/index.html

[110] William, Chris, "Guitarist for Metal Band Iced Earth Surrenders to FBI on Capitol Insurrection Charges," Variety (January 17, 2021) at https://variety.com/2021/music/news/metal-guitarist-john-schaffer-surrenders-fbi-capitol-siege-1234887239/

[111] *Ibid.*

[112] *Ibid.*

A dramatic photograph of Schaffer was among the first twenty-six still shots released January 7, 2021 by the DC Metro Police for "Persons of Interest in Unrest-Related Offenses."[113] In it, Schaffer is wearing a baseball cap that reads "Oath Keepers Lifetime Member."[114]

As quickly as January 10, 2021, four members of "Iced Earth" released a statement to separate themselves from Schaffer.[115] By February 15, those band members quit.[116] *But, hey!* The band still had nearly 500,000 followers on Facebook as of January 28.[117]

The Court has not yet announced Schaffer's sentence and fine (which it will determine), but, in the meantime, Judge Mehta granted requests for Schaffer to travel to visit family, his lawyers, and music studios in multiple states for recording sessions.[118] The charges to which Schaffer has plead carry a combined up to thirty years in federal prison and fines to $850,000. Not part of the DOJ Press Release of April 16? The DOJ instead recommends Schaffer serve only 41-51 months in prison.[119] Oddly, and only reported by the LA Times, the remark "Schaffer's deal with prosecutors may qualify him for the federal witness security program."[120] Protection "from who" was not defined; the article said nothing more than that.

---

[113] Metropolitan Police, Washington, D.C., "Persons of Interest in Unrest-Related Offenses" (January 7, 2021) at
https://mpdc.dc.gov/sites/default/files/dc/sites/mpdc/publication/attachments/POIs%20of%20Interest_1.7.21.pdf, see slide 15.

[114] *U.S. v. Schaffer*, Statement of Facts (January 16, 2021), p. 2.

[115] "Stu, Luke, Jake, Brent of ICED EARTH issues statement," Metal-Rules.com (January 10, 2021) at
https://www.metal-rules.com/2021/01/10/stu-luke-jake-brent-of-iced-earth-issues-statement/

[116] Divita, Joe, "Iced Earth singer Stu Block, Bassist Luke Appleton + Guitarist Jake Dreyer have quit the band," Loudwire (February 15, 2021) at https://loudwire.com/iced-earth-stu-block-luke-appleton-quit/

[117] Rosenberg, Axl, "Editorial: Will the Capitol Riot Actually Hurt Jon Schaffer's Career?" Metal Sucks (January 28, 2021) at https://www.metalsucks.net/2021/01/28/editorial-will-the-capitol-riot-actually-hurt-jon-schaffers-career/

[118] Walters, Greg, "Looks Like this Metal Guitarist who Stormed the Capitol just Turned on the Oath Keepers," LA Times (April 16, 2021) at https://www.vice.com/en/article/wx5q5w/capitol-riot-jon-ryan-schaffer-oath-keepers

[119] Hsu, Spencer and Barrett, Devlin, "Founding member of Oath Keepers enters first guilty plea in Jan. 6 Capitol breach," The Washington Post (April 16, 2021) at
https://www.washingtonpost.com/local/legal-issues/guilty-plea-capitol-riot/2021/04/16/f7d5d420-9eb6-11eb-9d05-ae06f4529ece_story.html

[120] *Ibid.*

The whole thing begs the question why Schaffer was even wearing an "Oath Keepers" baseball cap on January 6? Schaffer's typical gig is hair long and loose (and full of sweat during performances) or wrapped in a Willie Nelson style headscarf. Schaffer's political alignment was captured in a recorded interview: "If somebody cares enough about the facts then they would look deep enough into what I actually stand for, which is, really, ultimate freedom. I'm about as close to an anarchist as you can be. I'm not a fan of government. I'm not a fan of the left – they're just as ridiculous as the extreme right. (emphasis added)"[121]

"Anarchist" is hardly synonymous with "Oath Keepers," so what gives Jon?

"Stewart gives out hats."[122] It's a phrase I've read in several articles since the arrests began. For those who walk in Second Amendment circles, it's common knowledge Rhodes is the (singular) founder of Oath Keepers. The only arguable headliner affiliated with the group since inception has been one constitutional sheriff or another. Board Members and state chapter leadership have changed over time, not unlike any other organization. Look back to early, year-of-founding-local-press clippings from outlets like the *Las Vegas Review-Journal*, and you find coverage of a booth at a gun show and a couple guys in t-shirts.[123]

Among the dozen "Oath Keepers" defendants, Roberto Minuta received his Oath Keepers "lifetime member" baseball cap from Rhodes when Minuta re-opened his tattoo parlor, Casa di Dolore, on May 30, 2020 in defiance of an Executive Order issued by the New York Governor during the pandemic.[124] Hats are standard PR to angle a little earned media with a visual.

The inherent problem with an individual like Schaffer being linked to the Oath Keepers is the irretrievable nature of blame in the media. The more salacious of the DOJ allegations about January 6 have been broadcast around the globe, literally, and there isn't and won't be the kind of

---

[121] "Iced Earth: Jon Schaffer," Zombitrol Productions by Andrew Craig (January 7, 2019), 10:45 at https://soundcloud.com/governorandrew/iced-earth-jon-schaffer

[122] See, e.g., Indiana Oath Keepers stating Rhodes names some individuals "lifetime members" for publicity purposes, in Hsu for The Washington Post (April 16, 2021), *supra*.

[123] "Oath Keepers pledges to prevent dictatorship in United States," Las Vegas Review-Journal (October 18, 2009) at https://www.reviewjournal.com/news/oath-keepers-pledges-to-prevent-dictatorship-in-united-states/

[124] *U.S. v. Minuta,* Affd. Support Crim. Compl., *supra,* ¶19; and, see, Wu, Lina, "Tattoo shop reopens to defy state law," Times (June 3, 2020) at http://www.timeshudsonvalley.com/stories/tattoo-shop-reopens-to-defy-state-law,17657

in-depth reporting the developing legal situation demands. As one New Jersey newspaperman put it: "The Oath Keepers have become a face of the January 6th riots."[125]

Returning to Caldwell, Watkins, and Crowl, let's push a more in-depth analysis of these independent actors. Caldwell (the FBI man) thought little of tearing down Rhodes and the organization. I've already covered that going into January 6. *After* January 6, Caldwell's glorification of outright violence became his dominant theme. Consider these Facebook posts and messages by Caldwell on January 8, 2021:

- "…it was instinct to snatch up my American flag and race for yhe (*sic*) capitol steps with while (*sic*) the patriot stereos eere (*sic*) blasting the song "we're not gonna take it" and we were screaming along as one."[126]

- "Then the lying media said Trump supporters were breaking through barricades so i (*sic*) said if we're going to get blamed, might as well do it so I grabbed up my American flag and said let's take the damn capitol so people started surging forward and climbing the scaffolding outside so I said lets (*sic*) storm the place and hang the traitors."[127]

- "…the people in front of me broke throgh (*sic*) the doors and started duking it out with the pigs who broke and ran. Then we started stealing the cops (*sic*) riot shields a d (*sic*) throwing fire extinguishers through windows. It was a great time."[128]

- "If we'd had guns I guarantee we would have killed 100 politicians."[129]

Oddly, these and other statements are characterized by Caldwell's attorney as follows: "What the Government misunderstands is that Caldwell's language and personality center around his military

---

[125] Katz, Matt, "An Oath Keeper Did Security for the Capitol Rally. Now, He's a Republican Candidate for NJ Assembly," The Gothamist (April 9, 2021) at https://gothamist.com/news/an-oath-keeper-did-security-for-the-capitol-rally-now-hes-a-republican-candidate-for-nj-assembly

[126] *U.S. v. Caldwell,* Govt. Opp. Def. Motion Recon. Detention, *supra*, p. 9.

[127] *Ibid.*

[128] *Ibid.*

[129] *Ibid.*

career and his addiction to Hollywood" and that he's just one of "a bunch of ex-military guys trying to out-plan one another."[130]

Let's face it: who knows what the truth is about Caldwell. Everywhere he could post and text and call about his "role" on January 6 at the Capitol, Caldwell lied. Caldwell's use of the word "inside," for example, on Facebook, elicited a string of violent, written replies.[131] Caldwell's claims there would be "2 million,"[132] "1 million,"[133] and other grotesquely inflated numbers of persons at the Capitol on January 6, combined with language that the media was lying during live coverage on January 6, was bait to bring people to Washington so they wouldn't "miss out" on a historic event.[134]

Caldwell's lawyer claims his client is retired on full disability, has undergone multiple surgeries, needs medical attention and prescription medications, and grew worse in prison as his medical needs were not met.[135] "Moving, sitting for extended periods of time, lifting, carrying, and other physical activities are extremely painful and Caldwell is limited in his ability to engage in them."[136] He has PTSD, sleep apnea, a heart condition, and a degenerative left ankle. Caldwell is "prescribed, but has not been receiving, oxy-morphine for his spine pain, Lunesta for sleep issues, CPAP machine, Gabapentin DHRA, and hydrocortisone."[137] "[H]is physical limitations would have prevented him from forcibly entering any building or storming past any barrier."[138] Caldwell is "…now using a wheelchair to ambulate, and is in excruciating pain in his lower back and limbs."[139] Caldwell's own lawyer describes his bravado as "comical," particularly the part

---

[130] *U.S. v. Caldwell*, "Motion and Memorandum in Support of Reconsideration of Detention" (March 2, 2021), p. 20.

[131] *U.S. v. Caldwell, Crowl, and Watkins,* Affd. Support Amd. Crim. Compl., *supra,* ¶48(k); see, also, *U.S. v. Caldwell, Crowl, and Watkins,* Indictment, *supra,* ¶50.

[132] *Id.,* ¶48(b).

[133] *Id.,* ¶48(c).

[134] For example, in Watkins' mind: "If Trump activates the Insurrection Act, I'd hate to miss it." *U.S. v. Watkins,* Govt. Memo. Support Pre-Trial Detention, *supra,* p. 5.

[135] *U.S. v. Caldwell,* Memo Support Mot. Rvw. Detention Order, *supra,* ¶3

[136] *Ibid.*

[137] *Ibid.*

[138] *Id.,* ¶5.

[139] *U.S. v. Caldwell,* Mot./Memo. Support Reconsider. Detention, *supra,*

where Caldwell portrays himself "like actor Mel Gibson in the movie, The Patriot, picking up an American flag and leading the charge."[140]

Where does the truth lie in any of Caldwell's words or even those of his several attorneys?

Relative to Watkins, the problematic misassociation includes her rush to disavow the Oath Keepers. As soon as she had the microphone, Watkins told the court she had "disbanded" her so-called "militia unit" and planned to cancel her claimed membership in the Oath Keepers. "I have no desire to continue with people who say things like that."[141] It puts Watkins in the ironic position of isolating herself from anyone she was trying to affiliate with.

In Watkins' case, the remarks of at least one judge who denied her bail request indicate acceptance of the government allegations, stating "You are an active participant, organizer, leader of others in engaging in this kind of conduct. The material found at your home certainly suggests further potential for organizing and further potential for violence."[142] The reference to "material found at your home" included Watkins' copy of "The Anarchist's Cookbook" – a book available through Amazon.com and BN.com, the two largest booksellers in America.

But, for Watkins, as with Caldwell, individual denials and disavowals will neither stop the prosecution in the courtroom, nor the persecution in the media.

Media coverage pertaining to Oath Keepers defendants run akin to these chronological samples:

> ➤ January: "The formation, known as "Ranger File," is standard operating procedure for a combat team that is "stacking up" to breach a building – instantly recognizable to any U.S. soldier or Marine who served in Iraq and Afghanistan. It was a chilling sign that many at the vanguard of the mob that stormed the seat of American democracy either had military training or were trained by those who did."[143]

---

[140] *Id.*, p. 15.

[141] Kovac, Marc, "'We're done with that lifestyle': Ohio woman charged in Capitol riot to cancel Oath Keepers membership," The Columbus Dispatch (February 26, 2021) at https://www.dispatch.com/story/news/politics/state/2021/02/26/ohio-woman-charged-jan-6-capitol-riot-says-shes-disbanded-her-militia-group-and-cancel-oath-keepers/6836608002/

[142] Kovac for Columbus Dispatch, *supra*, quoting the Hon. Amit P. Mehta, D.C. District Court.

[143] Biesecker, Michael, Beliberg, Jake, and LaPorta, James, "Capitol Rioters Included Highly Trained Ex-Military and Cops," WBUR [Boston] (January 15, 2021) at https://www.wbur.org/news/2021/01/15/capitol-riot-military-police

> February: "A federal judge decided Friday that the alleged ringleader of the most serious paramilitary conspiracy stemming from the Capitol attack must stay in jail before trial. The ruling came during a federal court hearing where alleged Capitol rioter Jessica Watkins disavowed the right-wing Oath Keepers militia…"[144]

> March: "Oath Keepers members have positioned some of their defense strategy around recasting themselves as peacekeepers aligned with law enforcement before and during the siege, rather than the revolutionary-minded militants that prosecutors have alleged."[145]

> April: "Prosecutors highlight alleged Oath Keepers' wild ride and gun discussions in major Capitol riot case."[146]

As prosecutors at DOJ and agents at the FBI peddle their narrative to the courts, the media, and the public, the Oath Keepers are not even waging a media counter-point effort. The allegations have gone unanswered via their website or press release or e-blast to membership or social media posting. Neither has Oath Keepers hired an attorney or public relations firm to speak on their behalf. The only press remark that I noticed during this period was Rhodes to *The Washington Post* to say "If we actually intended to take over the Capitol, we'd have taken it, and we'd have brought guns."[147]

For anyone who has heard Rhodes speak or for anyone within Second Amendment activism circles or, truthfully, for any Veteran, LEO, or gun owner with any modicum of training, this comment by Rhodes is less offensive than it plays for non-politically engaged Americans. It is, simply: literal. But, it's not one that will protect the Oath Keepers brand, nor is it one that assists moderates and politically-unaffiliated persons to arrive at a comfort level with the organization.

---

[144] Cohen for CNN, *supra.*

[145] WENY News, "Roger Stone makes appearances in pair of Oath Keeper court filings" (March 19, 2021) at https://www.weny.com/story/43522301/roger-stone-makes-appearances-in-pair-of-oath-keeper-court-filings

[146] Polantz, Katelyn, "Prosecutors highlight alleged Oath Keepers' wild ride and gun discussions in major Capitol riot case, WENY News (April 9, 2021) at https://www.weny.com/story/43639019/prosecutors-highlight-alleged-oath-keepers-wild-ride-and-gun-discussions-in-major-capitol-riot-case

[147] Hsu, Spencer, "Oath Keepers founder, associates exchanged 19 calls from start of Jan. 6 riot through breach, prosecutors allege," The Washington Post (April 1, 2021) at https://www.washingtonpost.com/local/legal-issues/oath-keepers-calls-capitol-riot/2021/04/01/1b48aad4-9338-11eb-a74e-1f4cf89fd948_story.html

It also doesn't assist the "Oath Keeper" defendants, assuming one or more of them are within your response metric.

All of which adds up to the Second Amendment taking a PR beating.

The FBI and DOJ have been clever enough in their attack. They picked Rhodes because he is cerebral and symbolic. They selected the Oath Keepers due to its membership focus of Veterans, law enforcement, and first responders, while ignoring its origins of response to civilian emergency in circumstances of inadequate federal and local municipal response following Hurricane Katrina. The attorneys' and agents' use of words like "paramilitary" and "combat" and "combat training" conveniently overlook that not a single firearm was confiscated at the Capitol on January 6[148] and that the only shot fired was a Capitol Police officer shooting and killing civilian Ashli Babbitt. They've made it easy to get lost in the hundreds of photographs and videos and data dumps from electronics and social media companies – easy for the average person cooking dinner for their kids to forget that it's irrelevant to the charges whether any one of these twelve defendants were or were not members of the Oath Keepers. The very use of the word "conspiracy" by agents and lawyers, alike, is designed to confuse the public, while the most fundamental elements of pleading documents are lacking.

As this White Paper goes to press, Rhodes has not been charged, nor has the Oath Keepers as an organization. Neither can be for there is no crime of "domestic terrorism," although it doesn't restrict the FBI/DOJ from asserting other, chargeable crimes. Prosecutors have many other choices, if supported by evidence, but not pursuant to the "domestic terrorism" script attempting to be written by the FBI and the DOJ.

Regardless: the damage is done. Courtesy of an abuse of the judicial system for a "shock and awe" campaign, the FBI and the DOJ have created a fiction that Rhodes mounted a private army called "the Oath Keepers" to storm the Capitol on January 6 to disrupt a sacred process. And, in America, "military," "paramilitary," "militia" – all are words synonymous with "big, black, scary guns."

---

[148] Testimony, Jill Sanborn, Assistant Director, Counterterrorism Division, FBI, Senate Hearing (March 3, 2021), at 1:53.

*during a pre-trial **hearing***

"We do **not** have at this point someone explicitly saying: our plan is to enter the Capitol."

March 12, 2021
Kathryn L. Rakoczy, **Assistant U.S. Attorney**

*hearing: pre-trial request for release of Thomas Caldwell before the Hon. Amit P. Mehta, D.C. District Court*

***pre-trial release granted***

## B – THE CONGRESSIONAL HEARINGS

From February 24 to March 3, 2021, the House and the Senate conducted more than fifteen hours of public hearings, involving fifteen witnesses. The hearings bore no relationship to the FBI/DOJ criminal prosecutions. None of the witnesses were defendants or their attorneys, nor were there representatives from any of the organizations being put on trial through the criminal cases. The Congressional hearings focused on the security failures of January 6 and how to improve Member safety. Another round of hearings is now underway.

For me, the usefulness of the hearings was to identify those supporting "domestic terrorist" legislation, lists, and funding. It's why I slogged through the hearing footage, associated witness statements, reports, letters, media coverage, and witness backgrounds. My question was who, currently, in Washington has the stomach to put Americans on lists, side-by-side with disciples of Osama bin Laden and risk the same outcome of state-sponsored assassination?

Keep in mind that while "international terrorism" has been a crime for decades, "domestic terrorism" remains a definition, only, not a crime. No organization with even the most coordinated operations relative to the events of January 6 can be charged with a crime of "domestic terrorism."

This distinction between labels and criminality was lost in the linguistics melee of the hearings. Post-January 6 language was a bi-partisan blur of "Oath Keepers," "militia," "IIIers," "Proud Boys," "QAnon," "sovereign citizens," "anarchists," "white supremacists," "the KKK," "#boogaloos," and "terrorists." No one on the Hill appeared the least bit concerned to be educated or to speak with precision about targeted organizations, leaders, or social media hashtags.

Funnily enough, the one outlier to this atmosphere was, arguably, Christopher Wray, the current Director of the FBI. But, was Wray doing no more than sprinkling pretty words, given the concurrent actions by his agents, just up the street, in the DC Circuit courtroom of Judge Mehta?

Unfortunately, it appears that whether or not the FBI is publicly calling for "domestic terrorism" legislation, forces are converging to push it forward. Forces, who are perfectly content to catch the Oath Keepers in the crosshairs with the KKK. And, among the unpleasant surprises of this go-round of "forces," high up on the Hill, is Republican Senator Lindsay Graham (SC).

## 1 – The Line-Ups for the Congressional Hearings

If you have time to watch only one witness testimony, fire up the C-SPAN footage of the hearing with FBI Director Wray. It's about three hours and well worth your time and consideration. At the very least, though, take a moment to read through this listing of the Congressional hearings, for a quick Polaroid:

- U.S. House of Representatives, February 24, 2021 before the House Legislative Branch Subcommittee[149] – witnesses[150]:

    o Brett Blanton, Architect of the Capitol;

    o Ms. Farar Elliott, Curator, U.S. House of Representatives; and

    o Catherine Szpindor, Chief Administrative Officer.

- U.S. House of Representatives, February 25, 2021 before the House Legislative Branch Subcommittee[151] – witnesses[152]:

    o Timothy Blodgett, Acting Sergeant at Arms, U.S. House of Representatives; and,

    o Yogananda Pittman, Acting Chief of Police, U.S. Capitol Police.

- U.S. Senate, February 23, 2021 before the Rules and Homeland Security Committees[153] – witnesses[154]:

    o Carneysha C. Mendoza, Chief of Police, U.S. Capitol Police;

---

[149] On C-Span at: https://www.c-span.org/video/?509226-1/house-legislative-branch-subcommittee-hearing-january-6-attack-us-capitol [run time 1:42] - title of hearing "Health and Wellness of Employees and State of Damage and Preservation as a Result of the January 6 Insurrection."

[150] Witness written statements for the February 24 hearing are found at: https://docs.house.gov/Committee/Calendar/ByEvent.aspx?EventID=111233

[151] On C-Span at: https://www.c-span.org/video/?509246-1/house-legislative-branch-subcommittee-hearing-january-6-attack-us-capitol [run time 2:40] - title of hearing "U.S. Capitol Police and House Sergeant at Arms, Security Failures on January 6."

[152] Witness written statements for the February 24 hearing: https://docs.house.gov/Committee/Calendar/ByEvent.aspx?EventID=111235

[153] On C-Span at: https://www.c-span.org/video/?509061-1/senate-rules-homeland-security-committees-hearing-us-capitol-attack-day-1 [run time 3:52] - title of hearing "U.S. Capitol Attack, Day 1."

[154] Witness written statements for the February 25 hearing: https://www.rules.senate.gov/hearings/examining-the-january-6th-attack-on-the-us-capitol

- o Robert Contee, Acting Chief of Police, Metropolitan Police Department of the District of Columbia;

- o Steven Sund, Former Chief of Police, U.S. Capitol Police;

- o Michael Stenger, Former Sergeant at Arms and Doorkeeper for the U.S. Senate; and,

- o Paul Irving, Former Sergeant at Arms, U.S. House of Representatives.

- U.S. Senate, March 2, 2021, before the Judiciary Committee,[155] witness[156]:

    - o Christopher Wray, Director, Federal Bureau of Investigation.

- U.S. Senate, March 3, 2021, continuing before the Rules and Homeland Security Committees[157] – witnesses[158]:

    - o Jill Sanborn, Assistant Director, Counterterrorism Division, Federal Bureau of Investigation;

    - o Major General William J. Walker, Commanding General, District of Columbia National Guard;

    - o Robert Salesses, Senior Official Performing the Duties of the Assistant Secretary of Defense, Homeland Defense, and Global Security, Department of Defense; and,

    - o Melissa Smislova, Senior Official Performing the Duties of the Under Secretary, Office of Intelligence and Analysis, Department of Homeland Security.

---

[155] On C-Span at https://www.c-span.org/video/?509033-1/fbi-director-christopher-wray-testifies-january-6-capitol-attack [run time 3:40] - title of hearing "Oversight of the Federal Bureau of Investigation: the January 6 Insurrection, Domestic Terrorism, and Other Threats."

[156] Witness written statement for the March 2 hearing: https://www.judiciary.senate.gov/meetings/oversight-of-the-federal-bureau-of-investigation-the-january-6-insurrection-domestic-terrorism-and-other-threats

[157] On C-Span at: https://www.c-span.org/video/?509313-1/senate-rules-homeland-security-committees-hearing-us-capitol-attack-day-2-part-1 [run time 2:37] and https://www.c-span.org/video/?509313-4/senate-rules-homeland-security-committees-hearing-us-capitol-attack-day-2-part-2 [run time 1:19] - title of hearing "U.S. Capitol Attack, Day 2" (testimony uploaded as "Part 1" and "Part 2").

[158] Witness written statements for the March 3 hearing: https://www.rules.senate.gov/hearings/examining-the-january-6th-attack-on-the-us-capitol-part-ii

Also available is the write-up commissioned by House Speaker Nancy Pelosi (CA-12).[159] And, I note that there are pending reports from the Government Accounting Office ("GAO") in response to a letter dated January 7, 2021, signed by more than 100 Members of Congress,[160] along with a report from the Department of Homeland Security, Office of the Inspector General ("OIG")[161]. A U.S. Capitol Police internal report was apparently completed March 1, but has yet to be released to the public.[162]

## 2 – The Intelligence Run-Up to January 6

Let's do a run-through of hearings-related information about the intelligence run-up to January 6 on the ground. Top line? The general expectation across law enforcement and government intelligence prior to January 6 was that the day would be similar to the "Make America Great Again" rallies of November 14, 2020 and December 12, 2020. Expected was a large gathering with groups in-fighting among themselves. There was no claim at the hearings that prior to January 6 the Oath Keepers were expected to be at the Capitol on January 6.

Capitol Police Chief Steven Sund (resigned) described:

> "The assessment indicated that members of the Proud Boys, white supremacist groups, Antifa, and other extremist groups were expected to participate in the January 6th event and that they may be inclined to become violent."

and

> "At no time during the previous MAGA I or MAGA II events did the crowd attempt to storm or attack the Supreme Court building, or the

---

[159] "Task Force 1-6, Capitol Security Review" (dated March 5, 2021).

[160] Correspondence (dated January 7, 2021) to the Government Accountability Office from U.S. Representative Jason Crow (CO-6), *et al.,* at https://crow.house.gov/sites/crow.house.gov/files/GAO%20Letter%20re_%20Jan%206%20security%20lapses.pdf

[161] Press Report (dated January 15, 2021) issued by the U.S. Department of Homeland Security, Office of the Inspector General, see https://www.oig.dhs.gov/news/press-releases/2021/01152021/dhs-oig-review-dhs-roles-and-responsibilities-connection-january-6-2021-events-us-capitol

[162] Kaplan, Michael, "Capitol Police inspector general slams department's January 6 planning," CBS News (April 1, 2021), see https://www.cbsnews.com/news/capitol-riot-police-inspector-general-report/

> adjacent Capitol building, and based upon all available intelligence, nothing of that sort was expected to happen on January 6."[163, 164, 165]

Capitol Police "Daily Intelligence Reports" of January 4, 5, and 6 – *the very day at issue* – projected the probability of civil disobedience or arrests as "remote, highly improbable, or improbable."[166]

Contrary to speculation by Members of Congress and in the media, no one in Washington who testified projected the events of January 6. Not DHS Office of Intelligence & Analysis,[167] not the FBI,[168] not the Capitol Police,[169] nor DC-Metro Police,[170] nor the U.S. House Sergeant at Arms[171]. Also contrary to speculation, there was no indication, either before or after, that anyone illegally obtained floor plans for the Capitol or hacked the primary server.[172] Computers and laptops and wired network access were shut down to prevent unauthorized access in the House.[173] No firearms were recovered, nor firearms charges issued, relating to events of January 6.[174] And, the total damage done to eight objects within the collection of art and antiquities on display throughout the Capitol on the day was $25,000.[175] No figure was given for total structural damage.

---

[163] Letter, Former Chief of United States Capitol Police Steven Sund, to Speaker of the U.S. House, Nancy Pelosi (dated February 1, 2021), p. 2.

[164] Sund, Steven, Former Chief of United States Capitol Police, written statement, February 23, 2021, p. 3. {*N.B.:* there are subtle differences between Sund's letter to Pelosi and his written statement, but not of a material nature for purposes of this White Paper.}

[165] Sund, Steven, Former Chief of United States Capitol Police, testimony, February 23, 2021, at 1:45, 2:27, 2:58, 3:22.

[166] Blodgett, Timothy, U.S. House of Representatives, Acting Sergeant at Arms, written statement (February 25, 2021), p. 2.

[167] Smislova, Melissa, Acting Under Secretary, DHS Office of Intelligence & Analysis, testimony (March 3, 2021), at 1:44.

[168] Sanborn, Jill, Assistant Director, Counterterrorism Division, FBI, testimony (March 3, 2021), at 1:48.

[169] Pittman, Acting Chief, United States Capitol Police, written statement (February 25, 2021), p. 4.

[170] Contee, Robert, Former Acting Chief of Police, District of Columbia Metropolitan Police Department testimony (February 23, 2021), p. 2.

[171] Irving, Paul, Former Sergeant at Arms, U.S. House of Representatives, written statement (February 23, 2021), p. 2.

[172] Blanton, Brett, Architect of the Capitol, testimony (February 24, 2021), at 1:12.

[173] Szpindor, Catherine, Chief Administrative Officer, U.S. House of Representatives, written statement (February 24, 2021), p. 3.

[174] Sanborn (FBI), *supra*.

[175] Elliott, Farar, Curator, U.S. House of Representatives, testimony (February 24, 2021), at :22.

## 3 – The Changes in Analysis on January 3 + 5

Amidst the publicly-available materials, two clippings stand out. One from the U.S. Capitol Police. One from the FBI. The Capitol Police sentence comes from a memo of January 3. The FBI sentences come from a memo of January 5.

On Sunday, January 3, 2021, a Capitol Police employee named Jack Donohue wrote a fourth and final, internal memorandum, titled "Special Assessment" of the "Intelligence and Interagency Coordination Division." Back on page 13, he wrote, in part:

> "Unlike previous post-election protests, the targets of the pro-Trump supporters are not necessarily the counter-protesters as they were previously, but rather Congress itself is the target on the 6th."[176]

On Tuesday, January 5, 2021, in the evening, a "Situation Informational Report" was circulated by the Norfolk, Virginia office of the FBI. It included:

> "As of 5 January 2021, FBI Norfolk received information indicating calls for violence in response to 'unlawful lockdowns' to begin on 6 January 2021 in Washington, D.C. An online thread discussed specific calls for violence to include stating 'Be ready to fight. Congress needs to hear glass breaking, doors being kicked in, and blood from the BLM and Pantifa slave soldiers being spilled. Get violent. Stop calling this a march, or rally, or a protest. Go there ready for war. We get our President or we die. NOTHING else will achieve this goal.'"[177]

According to FBI Director Wray, this thread post was "raw, unverified, and uncorroborated."[178] According to FBI Assistant Director Sanborn, this was a "non-attributed message posted to a message board."[179] USCP Acting Chief Pittman quoted from the FBI document during the hearing: "This is an information report, not evaluated intelligence. It is being shared for information purposes, but has not been fully evaluated, integrated with other information,

---

[176] Pittman, written statement, *supra*, p. 2.

[177] Barrett, Devlin and Zapotosky, Matt, "FBI report warned of 'war' at Capitol, contradicting claims there was no indication of looming violence," The Washington Post (January 12, 2021) at https://www.washingtonpost.com/national-security/capitol-riot-fbi-intelligence/2021/01/12/30d12748-546b-11eb-a817-e5e7f8a406d6_story.html

[178] Wray, testimony, *supra*, at :32.

[179] Sanborn, testimony, *supra (Part II)*, at :21. At no point in the hearings or witness statements is the message board cited.

interpreted or analyzed. Receiving agencies are requested not to take action based on the raw reporting."[180]

Neither memo is available in full to the public, nor was either memo provided to Congress ahead of the hearings. However, these memoranda were apparently leaked to *The Washington Post* and partially published, in small excerpts, in articles on January 12 and 15.[181, 182] Each memo excerpt, as published, was confirmed during the hearings by USCP witnesses and FBI witnesses.[183] Acting Capitol Police Chief Pittman agreed to furnish the USCP memo to Congress.[184] FBI Director Wray committed only to "get with [his] staff" to discuss the request.[185]

It's a bit of a curiosity that the Capitol Police memo of January 3 was issued at all. Sund testified the Capitol Police have 30-35 officers in their Intelligence Division. He called Capitol Police a "consumer of intelligence" from the eighteen Executive Branch intelligence agencies. Sund said that while the Capitol Police does have the ability to look at open-source materials, they "do not collect in depth, specific intelligence."[186]

Without the documents to review, we can only look at the man behind it. The man behind the Capitol Police internal report was John K. ("Jack") Donohue, a man who may be propelling the Oath Keepers forward within national security circles. Since only November 2020, Donohue was hired to head the Capitol Police "Intelligence and Inter-Agency Coordination Division."[187]

Donahue appears to have singled-out the Oath Keepers prior to starting the position with Capitol Police. In 2020, Donahue worked concurrently for CyVision Technologies and for Rutgers University. At Rutgers, he co-authored a "Case Study on the Militia-Sphere" titled "COVID-19, Conspiracy and Contagious Sedition." The short paper looked at social media platforms with "…explosive memes about police brutality to calls for insurgency, state by state, against lockdown

---

[180] Pittman, testimony, *supra,* at 1:15.

[181] Barrett for The Washington Post (January 12, 2021), *supra.*

[182] Leonnig, Carol D., "Capitol Police intelligence report warned three days before attack that 'Congress itself' could be targeted," The Washington Post (January 15, 2021) at https://www.washingtonpost.com/politics/capitol-police-intelligence-warning/2021/01/15/c8b50744-5742-11eb-a08b-f1381ef3d207_story.html

[183] *N.B.:* not one Member asked the source of the leak from the law enforcement or agency directors or witnesses.

[184] Pittman, testimony, *supra,* at 1:38.

[185] Wray, testimony, *supra,* at :45.

[186] Sund, testimony, *supra,* at 3:37.

[187] *Ibid.*

orders."[188] One photograph in the report was captioned "convergence of the boogaloo meme and well-known anti-government extremist movements."[189] The words "Oath Keepers" appears three times in the report without any context, traditional analytics, or intelligence.[190] There is no methodology section to the paper to review what was done to account for bots, disinformation users, duplicate user accounts, spammers, or baiters.

The other reason the Capitol Police/Donohue memo stands out is because it <u>wasn't</u> discussed during the Congressional hearings. Multiple House and Senate Members railed on the FBI-Norfolk memo. The FBI-Norfolk memo was not supplied to Congress by the FBI. The author of the FBI-Norfolk memo was not identified. The individual who made the supposed chat board post was not identified. The chat board was not named. FBI Director Wray several times stated the chat post quoted in the FBI-Norfolk memo of January 5 was unvetted and unverified, and did not rise to the level of "intelligence." None of these factors stopped Members of the House and Senate from asking questions about the FBI-Norfolk memo. No comparable questions were asked about the USCP memo.

Rewind slightly. In July 2020, Donohue testified at a U.S. House of Representatives hearing on "Assessing the Threat from Accelerationists and Militia Extremists," including this from his written submission:

> "What is needed technologically is akin to a social media NORAD, a monitoring station that is technologically capable to generate finished intelligence rapidly and at a massive scale that can perceive imminent threats <u>before they emerge</u>, and detail them as the work at Rutgers and the Network Contagion Research Institute seeks to do with such tools. (emphasis added)"[191]

---

[188] Finkelstein, Joel, *et al.*, "COVID-19, Conspiracy and Contagious Sedition: A Case Study on the Militia-Sphere," Rutgers University (undated, circa July 2020), p. 4 at
https://networkcontagion.us/reports/covid-19-conspiracy-and-contagious-sedition-a-case-study-on-the-militia-sphere/ N.B.: The photograph is plagiarized, without attribute. It is sourced as a Getty Image by Karen Ducey, taken April 19, 2020 in Olympia, WA. Find at
https://www.gettyimages.com/detail/news-photo/matt-marshall-of-the-right-wing-group-washington-state-news-photo/1210404370

[189] *Ibid.*

[190] *Id.*, pp. 4, 7, and 13.

[191] Statement, John K. Donohue, Hearing on "Assessing the Threat from Accelerationists and Militia Extremists," U.S. House Committee on Homeland Security, Subcommittee on Intelligence and Counterterrorism (July 16, 2020), pp. 2-3
at https://homeland.house.gov/imo/media/doc/Testimony%20-%20Donohue.pdf

Given Sund's remarks about USCP being a "consumer" of intelligence, it begs a question (not asked during the hearings): what did Donahue use as the basis for his memorandum remark? Was it generated at Rutgers or another third-party and was it with or without contract or authorization?

As the record stands, Donohue's 2020 testimony around computer programming reads like NORAD personified and lying in a tank of water with the precogs from *Minority Report.* It's difficult to decide who is more fanciful or more disconcerting: Caldwell or Donohue.

Dial back even one tic further to the Rutgers/private contractor resume line of Donohue, and you'll read that he served on the FBI "Criminal Justice Information Systems Advisory Policy Board," including as its chair from 2016-2018. The Advisory Policy Board "is responsible for reviewing appropriate policy, technical, and operational issues related to CJIS Division programs,"[192] which, I should emphasize, <u>includes NICS</u>. Donohue claims credit for authoring reports on "privacy and access to information" for the FBI and the Department of Homeland Security.[193] Authorship of government reports could not be verified for purposes of this White Paper. Donohue served through his role of then employment with the New York City Police Department.

Donohue declined to speak to *The Washington Post* for the article on the leaked memo.[194] Likewise, Donohue did not testify in the recent hearings, nor did he submit a written statement.

## 4 – Analytics on the Ground on January 6

According to Former U.S. Capitol Police Chief Sund, he had no particular security concerns until word reached him on January 6 at 12:52 p.m. of the discovery of pipe bombs outside the RNC and DNC.[195] At almost the same time, Sund observed from his position in the Command Center a group that "…did not act like any group of protestors I had ever seen."[196] In his words:

---

[192] FBI website, "The CJIS Advisory Process" at https://www.fbi.gov/services/cjis/the-cjis-advisory-process

[193] "CyVision Technologies appoints Paul Goldenberg and John "Jack" Donohue to board of advisors," Security Magazine, August 21, 2020, at https://www.securitymagazine.com/articles/93128-cyvision-technologies-appoints-paul-goldenberg-and-john-jack-donohue-to-board-of-advisors

[194] Leonnig for The Washington Post (January 15, 2021), *supra.*

[195] Sund, written statement, *supra*, p. 6.

[196] *Id.,* p. 5.

> "As soon as this group arrived at our perimeter, they immediately began to fight violently with the officers and to tear apart the steel crowd control barriers, using them to assault the officers. It was immediately clear that their primary goal was to defeat our perimeter as quickly as possible and to get past the police line. This mob was like nothing I have seen in my law enforcement career. The group consisted of thousands of well-coordinated, well-equipped violent criminals. They had weapons, chemical munitions, protective equipment, explosives, and climbing gear. A number of them were wearing radio ear pieces indicating a high level of coordination."[197]

This was Sund's description for approximately 12:50 p.m. of a "deteriorating rapidly" situation.[198]

During his testimony, Sund stated that his order for the evacuation of the Capitol and the Library of Congress was issued upon his notification of the pipe bombs. Sund specifically stated that he did so prior to his witnessing of the group at the Capitol.[199]

In case you are wondering, the FBI/DOJ allegations put the movement of "the stack" of alleged Oath Keepers towards the Capitol building "at about 2:35 p.m."[200] – nearly ninety minutes after Sund says he saw "a group" arriving at the perimeter and fighting with law enforcement. The movements of the "Oath Keeper" defendants were so after-the-fact and impromptu as to involve the use of a hijacked golf cart by two defendants, Minuta and James, at approximately 2:30 p.m., to get from the Ellipse (site of the White House/Trump rally) to the Capitol.[201]

## 5 – A Convenient Political Target

Very few Americans have the stomach to talk about post-9/11 America, even twenty years later. Snatching people off sidewalks. CIA black sites in Europe. Enhanced Interrogation Techniques. Abu Ghraib. Guantanamo Bay. Pre-authorized kill lists. Unmanned drone assassinations, including of foreign nationals on their own soil. Dancing in the streets on Pennsylvania Avenue over the extermination of Osama bin Laden. Even Democrats have a surprising appetite for this flavor of violence, as long as it's abroad and picks off one foreigner at

---

[197] Sund, letter of February 12, 2021 to Pelosi, *supra*, p. 5. See, also, Sund, written statement, *supra*, p. 6.

[198] Sund, written statement, *ibid*.

[199] Sund, testimony, *supra*, at 2:09.

[200] *U.S. v. Caldwell, et al.*, Third Superseding Indictment, *supra*, ¶95.

[201] *Id.*, ¶91. *N.B.*: the distance is otherwise a forty-minute walk.

a time via joystick. We are the shining light upon the hill and the Constitution doesn't apply to foreigners. *Have we really killed over 8,500 using drone warfare since 2010?*[202] *It seems like just yesterday the drone was invented!*

Look back to the boilerplate language deployed by FBI Agents and DOJ Attorneys throughout the criminal cases. The Oath Keepers "...explicitly focus on recruiting current and former military, law enforcement, and first-responder personnel..." This is part of a narrative that Rhodes is a sort of Pied Piper, luring American's finest men and women of the Armed Services into a private army that could be turned against the country for which these men and women recently killed foreigners overseas.

Rhodes is easy to caricature into this part. A graduate of Yale Law School, the old Ivy that has always been for those radical free thinkers from otherwise good families. Hair never cut short enough. Posture never straight enough. Facial expression as laid back as someone from the Midwest (even though he's from the Southwest). That he was disbarred by the Montana Supreme Court, by default, adds to that just-bad-boy-enough-not-to-scare-the-average-voter.[203] You can put his face on the front page, above the fold, and it will intrigue people to say, "Who's that?"

Rhodes, himself, is a Veteran, but that detail doesn't easily suit him, either.

In 2004, after serving in the military and while at Yale Law School, Rhodes wrote a dissertation titled, "Solving the Puzzle of 'Enemy Combatant' Status."[204] Rhodes spent 94-pages on the academic question of jurisdiction of military tribunals versus civilian courts as the appropriate forum for the enemy combatant. While it may have won an award at Yale, an anonymous post to one of Rhodes' blogs about the paper pretty much summed up the mood of the country in 2006, five years post-9/11: "The guy was a terrorist so I am not too upset."[205]

Then, there's the "place" of Oath Keepers among various groups to the right of moderate gun owners. Neither the NRA, nor its state-affiliated chapters, are likely to jump up in any official

---

[202] "Drone Warfare," The Bureau of Investigative Journalism (September 4, 2020) at https://www.thebureauinvestigates.com/projects/drone-war

[203] Order, Supreme Court of the State of Montana, PR 14-0698 (December 8, 2015); find through https://directory.mt.gov/online-services

[204] Find the full dissertation at https://www.yumpu.com/en/document/read/35925676/solving-the-puzzle-of-enemy-combatant-status-oath-keepers

[205] Stewart Rhodes on blogspot.com, "Understanding Enemy Combatant Status and the Military Commissions Act, Part I" (October 28, 2006) at http://stewart-rhodes.blogspot.com/2006/10/enemy-combatant-status-no-more.html

capacity to defend the Oath Keepers or Rhodes, in spite of the NRA's origins relative to America's militia.[206] It is fair to say, culturally, those who have memberships to the NRA concurrently with any "other" groups (like Oath Keepers) are perceived as also possibly being members of a "militia" and not good for the big business of guns.[207]

By the time you get to the 2021 hearings, there's just this mish-mash of language that has been chugging along for the past twenty years. It's now amplified by more than a year of protests and riots. Already, throughout 2020, there was a culture war over use of the words "protestor," "rioter," and "criminal." On the day of January 6, the language overflowed from "protestor," to "rioter," to "the mob," to "insurrectionist." Concurrently, there was a push to elevate the U.S. Capitol as a much more sacred shrine than municipal (generic) city halls.

The FBI Director is thus heard to say at the hearings that within the FBI:

- they are trying to learn the "magic words;"
- with every arrest the FBI is learning about groups, means, methods, resources, and opportunities; and,
- within the FBI there is a separate nomenclature.[208]

The admitted ignorance of the FBI about the various domestic groups and individuals at the Capitol on January 6 feeds into its "answers" to (or "education of") Congress during the hearings and the judiciary during the lawsuits. To those with no experience with anything having to do with the Second Amendment Movement as distinct from everyone else who was at the Capitol on January 6, the hearings were a morass of hyperbole.

Let me say this. As concerns foreign terrorist organizations such as al'Qaeda, ISIS, and "ISIS-affiliates," I am less concerned with interchangeability. There is a unity of objective and similarity of means across these organizations.

By contrast, I am troubled by the current jumble of American group names and negative labels. Political philosophies are not synonymous among national organizations and groups and hash-taggers. You cannot (and should not) interchange NRA, militia, IIIers, Oath Keepers,

---

[206] The N.R.A. Book of Small Arms, Volume One, 1946, Second Printing 1948. "The National Rifle Association of America is seventy-five years old but for two-thirds of its existence it was known only to a couple of thousand people, mostly officers of the "militia" and a few Regulars, who believed that individual marksmanship was the foundation of soldierly training," Foreword by C.B. Lister, Secretary-Treasurer, NRA.

[207] Fiscal year ending December 2018 Form 990 filings list total annual revenue for the NRA as $352,550,864, using IRS search at https://apps.irs.gov/app/eos/allSearch

[208] Wray, FBI Director, testimony, *supra*, at 2:03.

sovereign citizens, anarchists, white supremacists, Proud Boys, Q-Anon, and Boogaloo Bois. They do not share the same origins, missions, or objectives. They do not share the same thoughts on activism. Most have nothing to do with actual Second Amendment advocacy. Several are nothing more than hashtags originating from 4chan, otherwise known as "cesspool of the Internet,"[209] and 8chan, known as "a go-to resource for violent extremists."[210]

The predictable destination of this word centrifuge is just plain "terrorist." Once there is a formal crime of "domestic terrorist" added to the existing "foreign terrorist," plus a list of each generated by the Secretary of State with the Secretary of the Treasury, the majority of Americans are not going take the time to make the verbal and written distinctions. When even Senator Graham is using "Oath Keepers" and the "KKK" in the same exchange with the Director of the FBI during public hearings, we are all aboard a freight train barreling towards linguistic simplicity.

The devolution into the single word – "terrorist" – will regress the FBI and DOJ, and with them our civil rights. Study history. Read about the persecutions of "Communists" during the McCarthy Era and prosecutions of "Socialists" during World War I. Find out what "COINTELPRO" stands for and how Labor Unions were sent fictitious letters to pit them against the Communist Party USA. America is about to do little more than repeat the worst of our intelligence failures, one label at a time.

> "Disturbingly, the boogaloo movement is at least the third example of a mass of memes escaping from 4chan to become a real-life radical political movement… (The conspiracy theory QAnon might be considered a fourth, but it is more than a political movement.)"
>
> The Atlantic, July 13, 2020
> "The Boogaloo Tipping Point: What happens when a meme becomes a terrorist movement"
> by Dale Beran

---

[209] Amadeo, Ron, "4chan founder Chris Poole leaves Google," Ars Technica (April 23, 2021) at https://arstechnica.com/gadgets/2021/04/4chan-founder-chris-poole-leaves-google/

[210] Roose, Kevin, "'Shut the Site Down,' Says the Creator of 8chan, a Megaphone for Gunmen," The New York Times (August 4, 2019) at https://www.nytimes.com/2019/08/04/technology/8chan-shooting-manifesto.html

## 6 – The Graham-Wray Exchange

Lindsey Graham has been a United States Senator since 2003, having first been elected to the House in 1994.[211] His official Senate biography page paints him as a protector of "our long-term national security interests" and a "leader in cutting spending."[212] His campaign website pitches him as "a leading advocate for cutting the out-of-control spending in Washington."[213] He's a lawyer, and was in both the Air Force and National Guard JAG Corps.[214] A minimal campaign fundraiser his entire political career, campaign contributions to Graham exploded in the 2020 re-election cycle to a staggering $107.7 million.[215, 216] The 2020 South Carolina race to re-elect Graham was the second most expensive Senate race in the U.S. at $239,824,140 total expenditures, including PACs.[217]

With this many more data points in mind, I'll say again: make the time to listen to FBI Director Wray's testimony. My second "at the very least" request is that you read through this 4-minute exchange between Wray and Graham. All underline and boldface are emphasis added by me. Be welcomed to grab your own highlighter.

> Graham:[218] Let's just stop there because we need to learn as much as we can from January the 6th. This is the 20th anniversary of 9/11. Are you concerned about international terrorists paying us a visit?
>
> Wray: Absolutely.
>
> Graham: <u>Are you concerned about the interaction between the international terrorists and domestic terrorists?</u>
>
> Wray: <u>That's a growing phenomenon</u>; certainly, something we're watching with concern.

---

[211] U.S. Senator Lindsey Graham, "Biography," on Senate.gov.

[212] *Ibid.*

[213] Lindsey Graham, campaign website, "Meet Lindsey Graham" at https://www.lindseygraham.com/

[214] U.S. Senator Graham, *supra*.

[215] OpenSecrets.org, "Sen. Lindsey Graham – Campaign Finance Summary" at https://www.opensecrets.org/members-of-congress/lindsey-graham/summary?cid=N00009975

[216] Federal Election Commission, Lindsey O. Graham, candidate for Senate, South Carolina, campaign ID S0SC00149 at https://www.fec.gov/data/candidate/S0SC00149/?cycle=2020&election_full=false

[217] OpenSecrets.org, "Most Expensive Races (Cycle 2020)" at https://www.opensecrets.org/elections-overview/most-expensive-races

[218] Wray, testimony, *supra,* this exchange begins at :56 (emphasis added).

Graham: One of my great concerns was that as people float into the Capitol with backpacks on, you had no idea who they were and what they were carrying, so it would have been very easy for some <u>international terrorist to infiltrate this crowd</u>. Do you agree with that?

Wray: I do think it would have been easy for that to happen. <u>I don't know that we've seen evidence that it did happen, but that's certainly one of the specific things we're looking for.</u>

Graham: After the attack, don't you think international groups are seeing this as a vulnerability in our system? {Wray asks Graham to repeat himself.} <u>International terrorist groups may have found a way to get closer to the Capitol by integrating themselves into domestic political movements</u>?

Wray: Well, certainly we think that the events on January 6 have been, at a minimum, an inspiration to a number of terrorist um-uh extremists out there, and it may even have been worse than that.

Graham: So, here's my challenge to you: sit down and put pen to paper and think big, not small, what do you need that you don't have, in terms of agents and resources and put it to paper. I'm on the Appropriations Committee with Senator Durbin – many of us here are. **I think we've got an opportunity here to plush you up**. Is it fair to say that since 9/11 domestic terrorism has exploded as a threat?

Wray: Well, it's certainly grown dramatically, uh –

Graham: "Grown dramatically," which takes resources to combat, is that correct?

Wray: Yes.

Graham: Has the FBI grown dramatically since 9/11?

Wray: Not as dramatically as the threat.

Graham: So, what I want you to do is take the number of agents and resources you had on 9/11 and tell us where you're at today, and make sure that we understand that the threats you are facing are much greater than they were twenty years ago, and challenge us to give you the resources to meet those threats. Back to January the 6th…

[Deleted are several questions concerning the FBI-Norfolk memo, covered above.]

Graham: Is the "Proud Boys" – they're a domestic terrorist group?

Wray: I don't think we have treated the <u>Proud Boys</u>, itself, as a domestic terrorism group, but we certainly have individuals –

Graham: What does it take to make the list?

Wray: Well, there is – uh, uh – as you may know – uh, Senator – uh under federal law – under US law – there is no uh "list" of domestic terrorism organizations the same way there is for foreign terrorist organizations.

Graham: Well, let's start to think about that in the next forty-seven seconds. Oath Keepers. Are they a domestic terrorist organization?

Wray: Again, as with Proud Boys, we have individuals who associate themselves with that group who are domestic –

Graham: Is Antifa a domestic terrorist organization? Same thing? Same answer?

Wray: Same answer.

Graham: So why don't we think about how to gather better information and expose some of these groups. **If they were on a list, would it make it easier for you**?

Wray: I think the issue of whether or not to designate or have a formal mechanism for designating domestic terror uh "groups" [makes hand symbols] in the same way we do with, say, al'Qaeda or ISIS – I think uh there's reasonable debate about whether or not it would really advance the --

Graham: Is the KKK a domestic terrorist group?

Wray: There is no uh legal designation for domestic terrorist groups --

Graham: **My point is I don't know if we should have one or not, but I think it's time to think about it**. [Graham raps the desk with his knuckles and ends his questions.]

In a matter of about six minutes on the clock, Senator Graham uses FBI Director Wray to advance the political agenda of passage of a "domestic terrorist" statute that would be the equivalent of the "foreign terrorist" statute. Graham equates Oath Keepers with al'Qaeda, ISIS, and the KKK. Graham. The same South Carolina Republican Senator who raised and spent all but $12,000 of the $107 million raised by his campaign on his 2020 race.

Should we be calling Rhodes the "Pied Piper" or "David?"

## 7 – The Fallacy of Equating an American Criminal to a Foreign Terrorist

Pause here to clear your head and get your bearings: al'Qaeda was responsible for the murder of 2,977 people in the 9/11 attacks.[219]

When you talk about "terrorism" on a global scale, the United States ranks 29th with just 39 total fatalities attributed to "terrorism" in 2019. Hardest hit population on the list: Afghanistan with 5,725 deaths in 2019 (one year) from terrorist attacks.[220] The deadliest groups around the world are Al-Shabaab, the Taliban, ISIS, and Boko Haram, in 2019 collectively killing nearly 10,000 people (one year).[221]

The only person who was killed during events at the Capitol on January 6 was Ashli Babbitt. The name of the officer who shot her was not released by Capitol Police. The officer does not appear to have resigned, nor has there been any public outcry for the officer to resign. There were no protests or riots over her death. The USCP internal investigation was closed with a finding of "insufficient evidence" without any mention whether the officer claimed to have given notice of an intention to discharge his firearm through closed doors.[222] The report was not released to the public and no one has gone to court to secure its release. According to a January 23, 2021 *The New York Times* article, the shooter was a "Capitol Police lieutenant" who had "31 rounds for his service weapon, and he has told others that he feared he might need them all."[223]

And, yet, in more than fifteen hours of hearings, only one witness uttered one sentence about the death of Babbitt. FBI Assistant Director Sanborn said, "I believe the only shots that were fired were the ones that resulted in the death of the – um – one lady."[224] No one spoke her name.

---

[219] See: 9/11 Memorial & Museum, on line at https://www.911memorial.org/visit/memorial

[220] https://www.visionofhumanity.org/maps/global-terrorism-index/#/

[221] "Global Terrorism Index 2020, published by the Institute for Economics & Peace, a Department of Homeland Security Center of Excellence at the University of Maryland, available at https://www.visionofhumanity.org/wp-content/uploads/2020/11/GTI-2020-web-1.pdf (see p. 18).

[222] United States Department of Justice, "Department of Justice Closes Investigation into the Death of Ashli Babbitt" (April 14, 2021) at https://www.justice.gov/usao-dc/pr/department-justice-closes-investigation-death-ashli-babbitt

[223] Goldman, Adam and Dewan, Shaila, "Inside the Deadly Capitol Shooting," The New York Times (January 23, 2021) at https://www.nytimes.com/2021/01/23/us/capitol-police-shooting-ashli-babbitt.html

[224] Sanborn, testimony, *supra*, at 1:53.

And, yet, in the couple hundred pages of written statements by fifteen witnesses, only one witness wrote one sentence about the death of Babbitt. USCP Acting Chief Pittman wrote "It was while Members were being evacuated that an insurrectionist was shot by a USCP officer outside of the House Floor."[225] No one wrote her name.

And, yet, there is the $107 million dollar man, Senator Graham, saying "I think we've got an opportunity here to plush you up," while he equates the Oath Keepers to al'Qaeda, ISIS, and the KKK.

---

[225] Pittman, written statement, *supra*, p. 5.

*in a* ▮▮▮▮ *memorandum*

"Individuals/Organizations named in this [situational information report] have been identified as participating in activities that are protected by the First Amendment to the U.S. Constitution. Their inclusion here is **not** intended to associate the protected activity with criminality or a threat to national security, or to infer that such protected activity itself violates federal law. **However**, based on known intelligence and/or specific historical observations, it is **possible** the protected activity **could** invite a violent reaction towards the subject individual or others in retaliation or with the goal of stopping the protected activity from occurring in the first instance. **In the event no** violent reaction occurs, FBI policy and federal law dictates that **no** further record be made of the protected activity."

Approved for Release: 5 January 2021
SIR Number: SIR-▮▮▮▮▮▮▮▮
Author: ▮▮▮▮▮▮▮▮
SOURCE: (FOUO)
FBI Field Office
Norfolk, Virginia

## C – "DOMESTIC TERRORIST" – IN A WORD. OR TWO

No one and no organization involved in the events of January 6 can be charged with a crime of "domestic terrorism." There is no such thing. "Domestic terrorism" exists only as a definition in the same federal statute where you will find "international terrorism." By contrast, "international terrorism" is a crime. You'll find this unique statute at 18 U.S.C. §2331.[226] After knowing what is contained at 18 U.S.C. §922(g),[227] you should familiarize yourself with the contents of 18 U.S.C. §2331. It is equally important.

Don't be duped into thinking a lil' ol' definition can't hurt us. It's not going to take a massive "Patriot Act" size bill to ignite these two words. Those two words – "domestic" + "terrorism" – are like an ICBM, sitting upright in a silo, the kind you've forgotten about since you were a teenager in the '80s. Once this missile leaves the silo, all the provisions of the Patriot Act will follow right behind the warhead.

If the demarcation of the civil rights of Americans on U.S. soil is eviscerated through passage of "domestic terrorism" crime legislation, it will be worse than a repeal of the Second Amendment. You think I am exaggerating? I am a licensed attorney, confident that whether through the sheer will of gun owners or the literal magnitude of the hundreds of millions of firearms already owned by individuals, in 2021, even the repeal of the Second Amendment would not end personal gun ownership. But: you permit the federal government to charge an American as a "domestic terrorist," seize all assets, suffer indefinite lack of charges filed or preliminary hearing, and potentially be snatched and hooded while walking down the street? Good luck. This law won't care one bit about "left" or "right." It will care only about the preservation of an insane consolidation of power in the Executive Branch.

The incident on January 6 was not a national security event. By a simple metric, it was nowhere near the scale of an al'Qaeda or ISIS or ISIS-affiliated attack relative to loss of life or property damage. By an over-simplification of a more complicated metric, the defendants charged thus far are not international terrorists seeking the annihilation of our republic. Even FBI Director

---

[226] 18 U.S.C. §2331 at https://www.govinfo.gov/content/pkg/USCODE-2009-title18/html/USCODE-2009-title18-partI-chap113B-sec2331.htm

[227] 18 U.S.C. §922(g) at https://www.govinfo.gov/content/pkg/USCODE-2011-title18/html/USCODE-2011-title18-partI-chap44-sec922.htm

Wray expressed the conclusion at the hearing that the majority of people at the Capitol on January 6 were simply swept up in it.[228]

Or, consider a very simple argument: it is legally unnecessary to activate a crime of "domestic terrorism." There is already a plethora of criminal laws with strict sentencing guidelines and financial penalties, as we covered in Section A. The January 6 defendants face multiple counts, carrying easily more than ten and in some cases more than twenty years in federal prison plus monetary fines. Some of these defendants, if convicted as charged, will literally age out and die in prison. The financial penalties and the attorney fees, if any, will also likely financially break others.

## 1 – The Statutory Origin of "International Terrorism"

It may surprise you to learn that the existing definition of "international terrorism," found at 18 U.S.C. §2331, was passed back in 1992.[229] It came into being through an innocuous, 5-page, federal courts administration act, co-sponsored by Sens. Chuck Grassley (IA, R) and Strom Thurmond (SC, ret., R). Its original purpose was to create the jurisdiction and venue for Americans to sue foreigners for acts of terrorism against a person or property. It was signed into law by President George H.W. Bush (R).

It reads, in current form, and without much amendment since adoption, as follows:

### §2331 – Definitions[230]

(1) the term "**international terrorism**" means activities that:

    (A) involve violent acts or acts dangerous to human life that are a violation of the criminal laws of the United States or of any State, or that would be a criminal violation if committed within the jurisdiction of the United States or of any State;

---

[228] Wray, testimony, *supra*, at 1:45.

[229] Pub. L. 102-572, "Federal Courts Administration Act of 1992" at
https://www.congress.gov/bill/102nd-congress/senate-bill/1569?q=%7B%22search%22%3A%5B%22cite%3APL102-572%22%5D%7D&s=1&r=1

[230] 18 USC §2331, *supra*.

(B) appear to be intended

    (i) to intimidate or coerce a civilian population;

    (ii) to influence the policy of a government by intimidation or coercion; or

    (iii) to affect the conduct of a government by mass destruction, assassination, or kidnapping; and

(C) occur primarily outside the territorial jurisdiction of the United States, or transcend national boundaries in terms of the means by which they are accomplished, the persons they appear intended to intimidate or coerce, or the locale in which their perpetrators operate or seek asylum.

Framed in the context of its enactment, the "international terrorism" definition almost feels nostalgic. The bad guys were somewhere "over there" and suing them (presumably *in abstentia*) in U.S. federal courts for money damages was a civilized way to deter crime against Americans and American financial interests abroad.

The big shift in the use of the legislation occurred during the Bush II Administration when Congress passed the infamous "Joint Resolution" on September 18, 2001[231] and the 150-plus page Patriot Act on October 26, 2001[232]. The Patriot Act was reauthorized three times, essentially, in 2005, 2010, and 2020, and it has undergone other provision-specific revisions to date.

> "[E]very Tuesday since Bush has been President it's been like a Mafia funeral around here. There are, like, fifteen cars with lights and sirens, and Cheney and Karl Rove come to the Republican caucus meetings and tell those guys what to do. It's all 'Yes, sir, yes, sir.' … In thirty-two years in the Senate, I have never seen a Congress roll over and play dead like this one."
>
> U.S. Sen. Arlen Specter (PA, 1930-2012)
> "Killing Habeas Corpus"
> The New Yorker, 12/4/2006

---

[231] S.J.Res.23, "Authorization for Use of Military Force" (2001-2002) at
https://www.congress.gov/bill/107th-congress/senate-joint-resolution/22

[232] Pub. L. 107-56, "Uniting and Strengthening America by Providing Appropriate Tools Required to Intercept and Obstruct Terrorism (USA Patriot Act) of 2001" at
https://www.congress.gov/bill/107th-congress/house-bill/3162?q=%7B%22search%22%3A%5B%22cite%3APL107-56%22%5D%7D&s=1&r=1

What started in 1992 as an ability to sue a foreign "terrorist" in an American federal court with all the usual litigation requirements morphed in 2001 into the singular power of the Secretary of State to nominate and designate a group as a "Foreign Terrorist Organization" ("FTO") and for the Secretary of the Treasury to block and seize assets, without any litigation requirements.[233]

The military spill-over of the elimination of Constitutional requirements surrounding an "international terrorist?" First, the targeting of "enemy combatants" in a manner consistent with, but without a declaration of, war, including indefinite detention and enhanced interrogation techniques. Second, the selective killing of individual foreign terrorists on foreign soil. Next, the judicially-sanctioned murder of a dual-citizenship Yemeni-American on foreign soil in accordance with a presidential, pre-authorized kill list.[234] Then, in case you missed this fly-by in 2010, the judicial and cultural acceptance of presidential pre-authorized kill lists growing to exceed 2,000 persons.[235] *Let's have a party on Pennsylvania Avenue to celebrate the extermination of Osama bin Laden in Pakistan in May 2011 by a Predator drone!*[236, 237]

Now, we are on the eve of these legal permissions being brought to bear against American citizens on U.S. soil. It's a progression "the right" frivolously orchestrated – and in other aspects profited from – supposedly in the name of "national security."

Yes, you are reading this section correctly. The "international terrorism" provision passed in 1992. The "domestic terrorism" amendment hit the books immediately following 9/11.

---

[233] See 8 U.S.C. §1189, "Designation of foreign terrorist organizations," discussed in Section D of this paper, at https://www.govinfo.gov/app/details/USCODE-2011-title8/USCODE-2011-title8-chap12-subchapII-partII-sec1189

[234] *Nasser Al-Aulaqi v. Obama, et al.*, 727 F.Supp.2d 1 (D.D.C., December 7, 2010) at https://ccrjustice.org/home/what-we-do/our-cases/ccr-and-aclu-v-ofac-al-aulaqi-v-obama

[235] A retrospective article can be found by Micah Zenko, "Targeted Killings and America's 'Kill Lists'," Council on Foreign Relations (October 6, 2011), at https://www.cfr.org/blog/targeted-killings-and-americas-kill-lists

[236] "Osama Bin Laden Dead" (May 2, 2011), The White House, at https://obamawhitehouse.archives.gov/blog/2011/05/02/osama-bin-laden-dead

[237] Harris, Elizabeth, "Amid Cheers, a Message: 'They Will Be Caught'," The New York Times (May 2, 2011) at https://www.nytimes.com/2011/05/02/nyregion/amid-cheers-a-message-they-will-be-caught.html

## 2 – Existing Statutory Definitions of "Domestic Terrorism"

"Domestic terrorism" means nearly the same thing as "international" or "foreign" terrorism. It is derived from Section 802 of the Patriot Act, and is found several lines below the "international terrorism" provision in 18 U.S.C. §2331, as follows:

**§2331 – Definitions**

(5) the term "**domestic terrorism**" means activities that

    (A) involve acts dangerous to human life that are a violation of the criminal laws of the United States or of any State;

    (B) appear to be intended

        (i) to intimidate or coerce a civilian population;

        (ii) to influence the policy of a government by intimidation or coercion; or

        (iii) to affect the conduct of a government by mass destruction, assassination, or kidnapping; and

    (C) occur primarily within the territorial jurisdiction of the United States.

"While the participants' actions on January 6 may be consistent with the definition of domestic terrorism, it is important to note that domestic terrorism is not a chargeable offense on its own. There is no federal criminal statute that establishes criminal penalties solely for "domestic terrorism…""[238]

Everything that legally surrounds "international" or "foreign" terrorism was constructed with the dormant "domestic terrorism" in tow. This statutory scheme (for which I can think of no comparable example) is sinister/brilliant. It's like installing a standard, duplex electrical outlet in the wall for the pair of lamps you just bought. You plug in one cord marked "foreign" and turn on the light. The other plug just sits in the wall, ready to accept the cord that says "domestic," on the matching lamp, as soon as you're ready to plug it in and turn it on. No extra work needed.

---

[238] Congressional Research Service, "Domestic Terrorism and the Attack on the U.S. Capitol" (January 13, 2021) at https://crsreports.congress.gov/product/details?prodcode=IN11573 *N.B.:* I do not want to confuse matters not relevant to our discussion, but §2331(5) can be an element of other federal crimes or may provide for an enhanced sentence. It's further into the weeds than we need to go for purposes of this White Paper, but I want to identify it as a touch-point for you.

Predictable results. Right where you left it. Available at a moment's notice without any further permits or contractors or inspectors.

A single-sentence bill could activate the provisions of the Patriot Act against Americans at home. It could also collapse the two words into the one-word term "terrorist," either concurrently or subsequently.

Where you already find that single word, "terrorism," defined, is within the Homeland Security Act of 2002,[239] codified at 6 U.S.C. §101(16),[240] as follows:

> (16) The term "**terrorism**" means any activity that
>
>> (A) involves an act that
>>
>>> (i) is dangerous to human life or potentially destructive of critical infrastructure or key resources; and
>>>
>>> (ii) is a violation of the criminal laws of the United States or of any State or other subdivision of the United States; and
>>
>> (B) appears to be intended
>>
>>> (i) to intimidate or coerce a civilian population;
>>>
>>> (ii) to influence the policy of a government by intimidation or coercion; or
>>>
>>> (iii) to affect the conduct of a government by mass destruction, assassination, or kidnapping; and
>>
>> (C) occur primarily within the territorial jurisdiction of the United States.

Alternatively, "terrorist activity" when committed by "aliens" is defined at 8 U.S.C. §1182(a)(3)(B)(ii), where you will find in the next paragraph what it means to "engage in terrorist activity".[241] Reading through this statutory definition of "to engage" is worth your attention for how soft laws could ensnare Americans, as follows:

> (iii) "**Engage in terrorist activity**" defined:
>
>> As used in this chapter, the term ''engage in terrorist activity'' means to commit, in an individual capacity or as a member of an organization, an act of terrorist activity or an act which the actor knows, or reasonably should know, affords

---

[239] Pub. L. 107-296, "Homeland Security Act of 2002" at https://www.govinfo.gov/content/pkg/USCODE-2011-title6/html/USCODE-2011-title6.htm

[240] 6 U.S.C. §101 at https://www.govinfo.gov/app/details/USCODE-2010-title6/USCODE-2010-title6-chap1-sec101

[241] 8 U.S.C. §1182 at https://www.govinfo.gov/content/pkg/USCODE-1994-title8/pdf/USCODE-1994-title8-chap11-subchapII_2-partII-sec1182.pdf

material support to any individual, organization, or government in conducting a terrorist activity at any time, including any of the following acts:

(I) The preparation or planning of a terrorist activity.

(II) The gathering of information on potential targets for terrorist activity.

(III) The providing of any type of material support, including a safe house, transportation, communications, funds, false identification, weapons, explosives, or training, to any individual the actor knows or has reason to believe has committed or plans to commit a terrorist activity.

(IV) The soliciting of funds or other things of value for terrorist activity or for any terrorist organization.

(V) The solicitation of any individual for membership in a terrorist organization, terrorist government, or to engage in a terrorist activity.

It's easy to say, "I would never give money to Boko Haram," but do you have a raffle ticket from a gun giveaway under a magnet on your refrigerator? A ticket stub from an annual dinner still in your wallet? And what if those are emblazoned with the "Oath Keepers" logo? And what if a defendant who paid for a hotel room and meals in D.C. gets reimbursed or used walkie talkies belonging to --?? Is it really so remote to think that you are only one steak dinner away from being served with a Criminal Complaint?

To give you a preview of how rapidly Executive Branch intelligence is moving towards the singular moniker of "terrorist," consider that in 2020, Congress directed the FBI and DHS to develop "standardized definitions of terminology relating to domestic terrorism and uniform methodologies for tracking incidents."[242, 243] The result was a three-page document listing these two statutes (above), and including that within DHS, the Office of Intelligence & Analysis uses the term "domestic terrorist" from a third source, its "Intelligence Oversight Guidelines",[244] as follows:

---

[242] Pub. L. 116-92, "National Defense Authorization Act for Fiscal Year 2020" at
https://www.congress.gov/bill/116th-congress/senate-bill/1790?s=1&r=1

[243] "Domestic Terrorism: Definitions, Terminology, and Methodology" (November 2020), jointly issued by the FBI and DHS, at https://www.fbi.gov/file-repository/fbi-dhs-domestic-terrorism-definitions-terminology-methodology.pdf/view

[244] Department of Homeland Security, Office of Intelligence and Analysis, Instruction IA-1000 "Intelligence Oversight Program and Guidelines" (issue date January 19, 2017) at https://www.dhs.gov/sites/default/files/publications/office-of-intelligence-and-analysis-intelligence-oversight-program-and-guidelines.pdf

L. **Domestic Terrorism**: Terrorism that is not international terrorism. (p. 44)

DD. **Terrorism**: Any activity that (1) involves an act that (a) is dangerous to human life or potentially destructive of critical infrastructure or key resources; and (b) is a violation of the criminal laws of the United States or of any State or other subdivision of the United States; and (2) appears to be intended (a) to intimidate or coerce a civilian population; (b) to influence the policy of a government by intimidation or coercion; or (c) to affect the conduct of a government by mass destruction, assassination, or kidnapping. (p. 47)

While there are some legislatively-small differences in the language, you get the point. Since 9/11, the intelligence agencies under the direction of four consecutive Presidents – both Republican and Democrat – have been developing linguistics around the terms "international (foreign) terrorist," "domestic terrorist," and "terrorist."

President Joseph R. Biden (D), in his State of the Union address of April 28, 2021, called the events of January 6 "The worst attack on our democracy since the Civil War."[245]

Now would be a convenient time to massage those inconvenient nuances before setting the whole thing in motion. Before plugging in the second cord to the existing outlet. So to speak.

## 3 – The FBI's Nomenclature and Analytics

The FBI has lead agency responsibility to investigate enumerated crimes within the statutory jurisdiction of the United States, which may involve "terrorist activities or acts in preparation of terrorist activities." Under a federal regulation found at 28 C.F.R. §0.85(l), "terrorism" is defined to include:

---

[245] "Remarks as Prepared for Delivery by President Biden – Address to a Joint Session of Congress" (April 28, 2021) at https://www.whitehouse.gov/briefing-room/speeches-remarks/2021/04/28/remarks-as-prepared-for-delivery-by-president-biden-address-to-a-joint-session-of-congress/

**28 C.F.R. §0.85 – General functions**

> (1) …the unlawful use of force and violence against persons or property to intimidate or coerce a government, the civilian population, or any segment thereof, in furtherance of political or social objectives.[246]

Or, as another FBI publication phrases it, "domestic terrorism" is "Americans attacking Americans based on U.S.-based extremist ideologies."[247]

To my ears, the "extremism" piece somewhat shapes itself into two parts: an ideology beyond majority views in a defined set of people + criminal activity (defined in the laws of the same set of people) to advance the ideology at the expense of others (within that same set of people). This may feel academic, but if you listen to a sufficient number of hours of intelligence agency – at this point FBI/DHS – testimony and press conferences, this is the succinct take-away.

The FBI currently uses "threat categories" to distinguish domestic threats or violence that rises to chargeable federal crimes, as follows:

- Racially or Ethnically Motivated Violent Extremism
- Anti-Government or Anti-Authority Violent Extremism
- Animal Rights/Environmental Violent Extremism
- Abortion-Related Violent Extremism; and,
- All Other Domestic Terrorism Threats.[248]

During the hearings, FBI Director Wray offered insight of two additional, internal phrases: the "homegrown violent extremist" ("HVE" by their own acronym) and the "domestic violent extremist" ("DVE"). The "homegrown violent extremist" he defined as "…inspired primarily by achieving global jihad, but not receiving individualized direction from [a] Foreign Terrorist Organization ("FTO")."[249] The "domestic violent extremist" he defined as committing violent acts in furtherance of ideological goals triggered by domestic influence, including, but not limited to, radical or ethnic bias, or anti-government or anti-authority sentiment.[250] Both the HVE and

---

[246] 28 C.F.R. §0.85 at https://www.govinfo.gov/app/details/CFR-2010-title28-vol1/CFR-2010-title28-vol1-sec0-85

[247] FBI Stories (archived), "Domestic Terrorism in the Post-9/11 Era" (September 7, 2009) at https://archives.fbi.gov/archives/news/stories/2009/september/domterror_090709

[248] FBI/DHS, "Domestic Terrorism: Definitions, Terminology, and Methodology," *supra*, p. 2.

[249] Wray, written statement, *supra*, p. 3.

[250] *Ibid.*

the DVE are, according to Wray, "…often motivated and inspired by a mix of socio-political, ideological, and personal grievances against their targets…"[251]

As per Wray's testimony, two quotes, about an hour apart:

> "The ideologies, if you will, that are motivating some of these violent extremists are less and less coherent, less and less linear, less and less easy to kind of pin down, and, in some cases, it seems like people coming up with their own sort of customized belief systems – a little bit of this, a little bit of that, maybe combined with some personal grievance of something that's happened in their own lives and that drives them. So, trying to get your arms around that is a real challenge."[252]

> "It used to be some angry, demented guy, living in Mom's basement (not that there's anything wrong with that) in one part of the country. [He's] now about to communicate with the similarly angry guy in grandma's attic in another part of the country, and they get each other spun up…"[253]

Wray's descriptions were superior to the allegations of his Field Agents in their Criminal Complaints. The FBI/DOJ legal documents contort themselves through hundreds of pages to warp around the words "Oath Keepers." It appears, however, that at least the leadership at the FBI is starting to realize the outdated concept of organized meetings driving violence. It's the counterpart of the same way DHS had to accept that nation-state geopolitical violence was outdated – a progression they didn't appreciate until after 9/11.

> DHS | "Post-9/11 developments in the online space…help people **see themselves** as part of communities and causes that transcend national borders, provide users with a sense of **intimacy** with people and groups half a world away, and **embolden** the adoption of identities or causes that may once have been obscure, marginalized, or otherwise unknown." | "Online extremist communities **lionize** attackers, encouraging others to follow their footsteps."
>
> DHS | "Strategic Framework for Countering Terrorism and Targeted Violence" | 09/2019

Director Wray's own testimony, just a few minutes later, in an exchange with a different Senator was to talk about "blended ideologies," ones in which a person holds a "customized belief system." Wray specifically said, "They don't have formal membership in an organization. They don't have clear command and control direction in a way that an al'Qaeda sleeper cell might have.

---

[251] *Ibid.*

[252] Wray, testimony, *supra*, at 1:06.

[253] *Id.*, at 2:00.

(emphasis added)"²⁵⁴  And, when later pushed by Senator Rafael E. ("Ted") Cruz (TX, R), FBI Director Wray described: "violence moves at the speed of social media," essentially connecting through a decentralized manner.  Wray observed: "The amount of angry, hateful, unspeakable, combative, violent even rhetoric on social media exceeds what anybody in their worst imagination [thinks] is out there."²⁵⁵

## 4 – How Does One Make the "Foreign Terrorist Organization List?"

How does one make the "Foreign Terrorist Organization List?"  Not through any process recognizable to a U.S. attorney as involving Due Process.  The simplest explanation to which I can direct you is a 29-page, single-spaced report from the Government Accountability Office titled "Combating Terrorism: Foreign Terrorist Organization Designation Process and U.S. Agency Enforcement Actions."²⁵⁶  And, the only good thing I have to say about "the FTO list" is that it is published.²⁵⁷

I don't want to go too far down the path of critical analysis of the designation and treatment of "Foreign Terrorist Organizations."  It's a different conversation and more about the stubborn question on the application of fundamental Constitutional concepts, like Due Process, to non-U.S. citizens, particularly in settings where we are the instigators of and primary actors in the resultant dynamic.

Instead, for our purposes in this White Paper, let's highlight one critical jog in the existing process, which is the pivot from intelligence agency investigation to the Secretary of State nomination.  I want to be sure you understand the gravity of this pivot point as it could play out against American organizations.

---

[254] *Id.,* at 1:15.

[255] *Id.,* at 2:03.

[256] U.S. Government Accountability Office, "Combating Terrorism: Foreign Terrorist Organization Designation Process and U.S. Agency Enforcement Actions" (June 2015) at https://www.gao.gov/assets/gao-15-629.pdf

[257] U.S. Department of State, Bureau of Counterterrorism, "Foreign Terrorist Organization" listed at https://www.state.gov/foreign-terrorist-organizations/ pursuant to 8 U.S.C. §1189.  For an introduction to these organizations, see the CIA World Factbook at https://www.cia.gov/the-world-factbook/references/terrorist-organizations/

Here's the rub: there is no requirement for notification that an organization or group is under investigation. The investigation process can take days, weeks, months, years – but, as soon as the Department of State is ready to strike, the Federal Register Notice requirement provides only thirty days for a nominee to get wind of the published notice and to timely and properly raise a legal objection and request judicial intervention in a court of competent jurisdiction.

Once notice has been published – and even before the deadline for the organization to object – the Secretary of the Treasury can take action to interrupt your financial operations. For however long the objection process may take. Even if you should ultimately prevail.

From 1997 (program inception) through 2019 (most recently reported data), the Department of the Treasury has blocked over $63 million of foreign terrorist assets.[258] When you consider that *Forbes* magazine published an in-depth article in 2018 on the ten wealthiest global terrorist organization with assets into the billions of dollars[259] (yes, with a "b"), it makes the Treasury numbers appear a bit, well, *lackluster*.

Instead of a profitability analysis, reconsider how you measure the impact of the "Foreign Terrorist Organization" designation. The designation also criminalizes the engagement of U.S. corporations, organizations, and individuals with the foreign terrorists.

The best way to illustrate this relationship to Second Amendment issues is to run a classic law school styled hypothetical. Pretend, if you will, that domestic terrorist equivalents are authorized and United States Secretary of State Antony Blinken nominates the NRA to the newly-minted "DTO" list basis "classified information" uncovered during the course of the current and on-going investigation of the NRA by New York Attorney General Letitia James.

Were you paying attention in Section A when I quoted the IRS Form 990 yearly gross receipts for the NRA? Fill it in here; $\_\_\_\_,\_\_\_\_,\_\_\_\_. Then, away we go, using this scenario, to its natural conclusion.

"Upon notification…the Secretary of the Treasury may require United States financial institutions possessing or controlling any assets of any foreign [or "domestic" – for purposes of

---

[258] U.S. Department of the Treasury, "Terrorist Assets Report: Calendar Year 2019," at https://home.treasury.gov/system/files/126/tar2019_0.pdf

[259] Zehorai, Itai, "The Richest Terror Organizations in the World," Forbes (January 24, 2018) at https://www.forbes.com/sites/forbesinternational/2018/01/24/the-richest-terror-organizations-in-the-world/?sh=a27fee07fd17

our hypothetical] organization included in the notification to block all financial transactions involving those assets until further directive from either the Secretary of the Treasury, Act of Congress, or order of court. (emphasis added)"[260] And that "classified information" considered by the Secretary in making the designation? "Classified information shall not be subject to disclosure for such time as it remains classified, except that such information may be disclosed to a court *ex parte* and in camera for purposes of judicial review under subsection (c)."[261] The judicial review of designation in "(c)" must be sought no later than 30 days after publication in the Federal Register.[262]

In plain English: in our hypothetical, the NRA collapses, financially, while waiting for judicial review of classified materials it will not have a right to see. Disagree? Don't tell me that $352 million in annual revenue isn't enough of an incentive for an agency to make the kill, while justifying its existence in the process.

The reality dimension to fuse into our hypothetical is that while Rhodes may not understand the game of corporate damage control, the NRA does. And it does with fabulous money, fantastic membership numbers, killer NRA-ILA alerts that mobilize people with voices and telephones and little black books of contacts. And that is what gets an organization to the level of survivability akin to J&J surviving the Tylenol deaths in 1982 and blood clot deaths in 2021. Too big to fail. Too beloved to besmirch. It also makes Oath Keepers something akin to collateral damage.

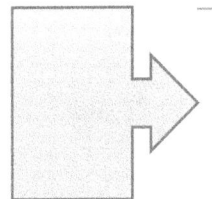

"In short, **without** the full **due process** afforded in criminal cases, the U.S. government can **bankrupt** political organizations it **asserts** are involved in domestic terrorism."

American Civil Liberties Union
"How the USA Patriot Act Redefines "Domestic Terrorism""
2021

---

[260] 8 USC §1189(a)(2)(B).

[261] 8 USC §1189(a)(3)(B) and §1189(c)(2).

[262] 8 U.S.C. §1189(c)(1).

Still not with me on the hypothetical?  Okay; forget *The Paper Chase*.[263]  Switch to the real-world case study of "Operation Choke Point."

The Federal Deposit Insurance Corporation ("FDIC"), as you may be aware, rates banks, and one of those rating criteria is the risk level inherent to the commerce engaged in by their customers.  In 2013, FDIC attorneys and DOJ attorneys began sharing rating and investigatory information to develop a list of "high-risk merchants" and a guidance document to attach to a subpoena served upon more than fifty banks and payment processors.

On the list of "Higher Potential Risk Merchants/Activities" was added "ammunition sales" and "firearms/fireworks sales."[264]  There was no data to support the inclusion of these consumer products on the list; just the casual key strokes and the opinion of an employee at a computer.[265]

As but one example of how this played out, consider this language from a bank compliance officers training program conducted by FIS Global, "a leading provider of technology solutions for merchants, banks and capital markets firms globally."[266]  FIS Global is a Fortune 500 company and is publicly traded.[267]  From their 2014 bank officers training program:  "Arms and Ammunition Dealers are identified as higher risk businesses <u>because they have a higher risk of being associated with terrorism and terrorist acts</u>. (emphasis added)"[268]

The House oversight hearing reports literally listed by name and retail location several firearms and ammunitions dealers holding valid Federal Firearms Licenses from the Bureau of Alcohol, Tobacco, Firearms and Explosives ("ATF") that were unable to conduct routine financial transactions, such as credit card sales, as a direct result of this FDIC/DOJ illegal adventure.[269]

---

[263] Bridges, James (Director). 1973. *The Paper Chase* [Film].  Thompson-Paul Productions/Twentieth Century Fox.

[264] Federal Deposit and Insurance Company, "Supervisory Insights," Vol. 8, Issue 1 (Summer 2011), p. 7 at https://www.fdic.gov/regulations/examinations/supervisory/insights/sisum11/index.html

[265] U.S. House of Representatives, Committee on Oversight and Government Reform, "Staff Report: Federal Deposit Insurance Corporation's Involvement in Operation Choke Point" (December 8, 2014) at https://republicans-oversight.house.gov/wp-content/uploads/2014/12/Staff-Report-FDIC-and-Operation-Choke-Point-12-8-2014.pdf

[266] See https://www.fisglobal.com/en/about-us and https://www.investor.fisglobal.com/

[267] *Ibid.*

[268] Staff Report (2014), *Id.,* p. 7.

[269] U.S. House, Oversight, Staff Report December 2014, *supra,* pp. 19-20.

As per one of the U.S. House oversight hearing reports on "Operation Choke Point:"

> "The inclusion of the FDIC guidance in DOJ's subpoenas effectively "weaponized" the high-risk merchants list. The implication was clear: banks were compelled to remove those clients from their portfolios, or risk a federal investigation by the Department of Justice."[270]

Key findings of an affiliated U.S. House report include that "Operation Choke Point" was designed to deny legal businesses access to banking and payment networks critical to commerce and that the DOJ lacked adequate legal authority for the initiative.[271]

The concept is known as "de-risking," and it occurs when a financial institution terminates or restricts business relationships to avoid perceived or actual regulatory risk, not otherwise in response to actual illegal activity.

While "Operation Choke Point" may have turned into an embarrassing blunder for the FDIC and the DOJ, and particularly their in-house counsel, we continue to see de-risking behavior among financial institutions and other companies, even as relates to the events of January 6 and people and organizations that may (or may not) have criminal liability. Most recently, Bank of America conducted an internal records review and simply "handed over customer data" to the FBI on customers who made purchases "of weapons or at a weapons-related merchant" between January 7 and an "upcoming suspected stay in D.C. area around Inauguration Day."[272]

Other recent headlines over terminated financial relationships:

- "Kroger unwittingly contributed to Indiana militia group Oath Keepers, grocer pledges review of support to nonprofits."[273]

---

[270] *Id.*, p. 17.

[271] U.S. House of Representatives, Committee on Oversight and Government Reform, "Staff Report: The Department of Justice's "Operation Choke Point": Illegally Choking Off Legitimate Businesses" (May 29, 2014) at https://republicans-oversight.house.gov/wp-content/uploads/2014/05/Staff-Report-Operation-Choke-Point1.pdf

[272] Carlson, Tucker, "Bank of America handed over customer data to feds following Capitol riot," Fox News (February 4, 2021) at https://www.foxnews.com/opinion/tucker-carlson-bank-of-america-customer-data-feds-capitol-riot

[273] Kroger is based in Cincinnati, Ohio. The headline is taken from The Cincinnati Enquirer (January 19, 2021) at https://www.cincinnati.com/story/money/2021/01/19/kroger-unwittingly-contributed-indiana-militia-group/4221388001/

- o *N.B.*: Indiana Oath Keepers is a IRS §501(c)(3) non-profit organization,[274] meaning it is recognized as such by the IRS, and is an Indiana-registered business entity separate from the national Oath Keepers[275].

- "Amazon boots Indiana Oath Keepers, 4 other militia-type groups from 'Smile' charity program."
    - o *N.B.:* The cited basis is the Amazon "Participation Agreement," the terms of which excludes from "Eligible Organizations" those non-profits that engage in, support, encourage, or promote "hate, terrorism, or violence."[276]

There will be those who will jump, prematurely even ahead of criminal convictions in a U.S. court of law, in the name of "protecting investors" and being "good corporate citizens." How big and how early is also part of the read of what's happening on the Hill as their people get tipped by government staffers of what's coming down the pike.

---

[274] IRS Tax Exempt Organization Search at https://apps.irs.gov/app/eos/detailsPage?ein=821498838&name=Indiana%20Oath%20Keepers%20Inc.&city=Westfield&state=IN&countryAbbr=US&dba=&type=CHARITIES,%20DETERMINATIONLETTERS,%20EPOSTCARD&orgTags=CHARITIES&orgTags=DETERMINATIONLETTERS&orgTags=EPOSTCARD

[275] Indiana Business Details at https://bsd.sos.in.gov/PublicBusinessSearch/BusinessInformationFromIndex

[276] Amazon, "AmazonSmile Participation Agreement" (updated October 26, 2020) at https://org.amazon.com/agreement?ascsubtag=[]vg[p]22012681[t]w[r]google.com[d]D

## 5 – Who Might Make the Initial "Domestic Terrorist Organization" List?

In all probability, if "domestic terrorist" legislation passes, we may expect to see a direct import of the list published for many years by the Southern Poverty Law Center as either "the" list or substantially close to the list.[277] Southern Poverty Law Center publishes the most frequently cited and the longest-standing list-keeping of domestic organizations, groups, and individuals of which I am aware.[278]

On the Southern Poverty Law Center list of "extremist" actors is the Oath Keepers. Their accompanying description is "…a compendium of much-feared but entirely imaginary threats from the government, including forcing Americans into detention camps, imposing martial law, and disarming all civilians."[279] The Southern Poverty Law Center, in its own rush to judge the Oath Keepers, rewrites U.S. history, denying such events happened or could happen again. Have they never heard of Fred Toyosaburo Korematsu?[280] The *writ of habeas corpus*?[281] Senator Feinstein's remarks, speaking of Mr. & Mrs. America?[282]

We would be kidding ourselves to think that if "domestic terrorist" legislation is enacted that the federal government will conclude its list-making at the Oath Keepers. That Rhodes is the

---

[277] See Southern Poverty Law Center "Groups" list at https://www.splcenter.org/fighting-hate/extremist-files/groups

[278] Additionally, the Anti-Defamation League publishes an extensive "Hate on Display" database, see https://www.adl.org/hate-symbols

[279] See, Southern Poverty Law Center, "Oath Keepers" page at https://www.splcenter.org/fighting-hate/extremist-files/group/oath-keepers

[280] See, *Korematsu v. U.S.*, 323 U.S. 214 (1944) and Executive Order 9066 (February 19, 1942) under President Theodore Roosevelt (R) at https://www.archives.gov/historical-docs/todays-doc/?dod-date=219

[281] See "A Proclamation" (General Orders No. 141, September 25, 1862) and "An Act Relating to Habeas Corpus, and Regulating Judicial Proceedings in Certain Cases," 12 Stat. 755 (1863) both under President Abraham Lincoln (R); "Proclamation Suspending Habeas Corpus" (October 17, 1871) under President Ulysses S. Grant (R); the "Military Commissions Act," 120 Stat. 2600 (2006) under President George W. Bush (R).

[282] 60 Minutes (February 5, 1995) interview of U.S. Senator Dianne Feinstein (CA, D) quoted to say "If I could have gotten 51 votes in the Senate of the United States for an outright ban, picking up every one of them – Mr. and Mrs. America, turn them all in – I would have done it."; see, also, as a legislative example, S.1034, "Assault Weapons Ban Reauthorization Act of 2003" at https://www.congress.gov/bill/108th-congress/senate-bill/1034/text

definitive "terrorist." And that as long as a defense attorney can distinguish "me" from "him" ("*him*" being Rhodes), then "my" civil rights are secure. No. It doesn't work that way. It's an exceptionally bad habit that Americans have: the police can be storming your next-door neighbor and you say '*that's my next-door neighbor,*' as opposed to '*that's my next-door neighbor!*' If the FBI, DOJ, and Congress are after the Oath Keepers, "militia," and IIIers, they are at our front door as gun owners.

We knew already, years ago, that even if "domestic terrorism" was not a separately chargeable offense, an American could be labeled a "terrorist" for FBI/DHS purposes and be added to the "Terrorist Screening Database" ("TSDB").[283] While the ACLU has been fighting the TSDB and the "No-Fly" subset list since 9/11, unfortunately their plaintiffs have been repeatedly dismissed for lack of a plaintiff with "standing," both a specific injury and a connection to the U.S. government. The arguments against intelligence agency labeling originate decades ago, to the old days of VGTOF and COINTELPRO[284] to the Communist Party USA and the Socialist Workers Party of America. Now the modern TSDB is a list specifically relevant to gun owners.

From 2015 - 2018, I had the privilege to represent dozens of plaintiffs, including Fulton County NY Oath Keepers and several individual members of the New York Oath Keepers, in a federal lawsuit against the U.S. Attorney General, the FBI, the Terrorist Screening Center ("TSC"), and the Bureau of Alcohol, Tobacco, Firearms, and Explosives ("BATFE" or "the ATF"). The case was *Robinson v. Sessions,* and it reached its completion when the U.S. Supreme Court declined to hear our appeal.

Most unusual, in the *Robinson v. Sessions* federal civil rights litigation, there were no material facts in dispute in the case. The Respondents admitted that they investigate every firearms customer as a potential "terrorist" through the Terrorist Screening Database ("TSDB") every time an ATF Form 4473 is filled out at an FFL for the purchase of a firearm. As I phrased it:

> The Respondents have placed "…the legitimate force of its
> criminal enforcement power…" behind the label of "terrorist" and
> hoisted it upon the American gun owner. *Meese v. Keene,* 481 U.S.
> 465, 477 (1987). This case does not relate to 50 U.S.C. §1881a
> ("Section 702," the FISA/FISA Amendments Act provisions about

---

[283] See, also, *Latif v. Sessions,* case 3:10-cv-0075, specifically, "Exhibit A," the March 2013 "Watchlisting Guidance" issued by the U.S. National Counterterrorism Center at https://www.aclu.org/sites/default/files/field_document/208-1.%20Handeyside%20Declaration_Exhibit%20A%204.17.2015_0.pdf

[284] See, FBI FOIA documents on line, specifically https://vault.fbi.gov/cointel-pro

> intelligence-gathering activities on foreign operatives abroad). This NICS-to-TSDB connection has nothing to do with "non-U.S. persons located abroad." *Clapper v. Amnesty Int'l. USA,* 568 U.S. \_\_\_\_\_, 133 S.Ct. 1138, 1144 (2013); 50 U.S.C. §1881a(d)(1)(A)-(B). It amounts to domestic spying.[285]

That the disqualifying factors for the purchase of a firearm at 18 U.S.C. §922(g)(1)-(9) do not include being listed in the TSDB as an alleged "terrorist" was not a popular argument to make before the Second Circuit Court of Appeals in New York City. Legally correct. But, situationally? Unpopular. The courthouse is physically located walking distance from the site of the former Twin Towers. It couldn't be helped. In 2017, the NICS-to-TSDB connection was the newest form of government-acknowledged domestic surveillance and it was the subject of our case. The Plaintiffs lived in New York and were concentrated in the WDNY District Court jurisdiction. This meant the Second Circuit Court of Appeals had appellate jurisdiction.

Congress had already, for more than ten years, rejected proposed legislation to prevent individuals on the TSDB from purchasing a firearm.[286] But even Congress couldn't stop the ATF, in conjunction with the TSC, from running every person submitting an ATF Form 4473 for a NICS background check being compared against the "Terrorist Screening Database."

You may only be familiar with the "No Fly List." That's a subset of the TSDB – a database that by best estimates in 2005 – includes 2.5 million names.[287] There is no due process requirement to provide notification of being placed upon the list. According to the DOJ, back in 1996, the year after the "Violent Gangs and Terrorist Organizations File" ("VGTOF") started, there were 445 groups and 180 individuals on the list.[288] Compare the recent 2.5 million TSDB figure against the roughly 65 total organizations on the "Foreign Terrorist Organization List." 2.5 million TSDB

---

[285] *Robinson, et al. v. Sessions,* Brief and Special Appendix for Plaintiffs-Appellants (June 16, 2017), p. 17 [17-1427-cv].

[286] See, e.g., "Denying Firearms and Explosives to Dangerous Terrorists Act" (S.551 2007-2015), "NRA Members' Gun Safety Act of 2013" (H.R.21), "Terrorist Apprehension and Record Retention Act of 2005" (H.R.1225/S.578), and "Preserving Records of Terrorists & Criminals Transactions Act" (S.2935, S.2820).

[287] Congressional Research Service, "Terrorist Screening and Brady Background Checks for Firearms" (July 25, 2005), p. 2; and, Congressional Research Service, "Terrorist Identification, Screening, and Tracking under Homeland Security Presidential Directive 6" (April 21, 2004), p. 31.

[288] Episcopo, Peter and Moor, Darrin, "The Violent Gang and Terrorist Organizations File," FBI Law Enforcement Bulletin, Vol. 65, Issue 10 (October 1996) at https://leb.fbi.gov/file-repository/archives/october-1996.pdf/view

versus 68 FTO. Unknown who or how many Americans are in the TSDB. (Got enough fingers and toes to follow all these digits?)

We had commenced the lawsuit at a time, December 2015, when the New York Daily News put NRA then-CEO Wayne LaPierre on its front cover along with several mass murderers, calling all of them "terrorists" and accusing the NRA of a "sick gun jihad against America in the name of profit."[289]

The day before my oral arguments at the Second Circuit, in November 2017, a man committed mass murder at Sutherland Spring Church. Oral arguments began with one of the three judges on the appellate panel asking me questions about that man's ability to purchase firearms when he should have been disqualified from making the purchase.[290] It was legally irrelevant to our case. The statute of disqualifying factors at 18 U.S.C. §922(g) was not being challenged in our case. It threw off the room and no one enforced the red light.

The Court subsequently issued its written decision as a "Summary Order." It directed the Clerk not publish the decision in the official reporter series. It is a public decision, but it has no citation in the official Federal Reporter Series. It is thus invisible, and, with it, what the Court did.

The judicial decision says, for example:

> "The Brady Act provides the Government with the authority to access any search criteria that will enable it to determine whether a prospective purchaser is prohibited by the Gun Control Act from purchasing a firearm. (citations omitted) Incorporating the TSDB into the NICS Background Check protocol <u>is merely one method that the Government may use</u> to determine whether a prospective purchaser possesses a disqualifying attribute. (emphasis added, p. 6)"

That underlined bit is legally incorrect. For more than ten years in a row preceding our case, Congress expressly declined to add a person's status on the TSDB as a disqualifying factor for the purchase of a firearm. They did so because no one knows how a person gets onto the list, no one

---

[289] *N.B.:* I was unable to locate a NY Daily News website copy of this issue/article on its website. It is available at https://nationalpost.com/news/world/new-york-daily-news-compares-nra-official-to-mass-shooting-terrorists-for-enabling-sick-gun-jihad

[290] Rosenberg, Eli, *et al.*, "Who is Devin Patrick Kelley, the gunman officials say killed churchgoers in Sutherland Springs, Tex.?" Washington Post (November 6, 2017) at https://www.washingtonpost.com/news/morning-mix/wp/2017/11/06/who-is-devin-patrick-kelley-gunman-who-officials-say-killed-churchgoers-in-sutherland-springs/

> **FBI Processing of Domestic Terrorists**
>
> "The FBI's Terrorist Review and Examination Unit ("TREX") receives requests **from FBI agents** to include individuals with **known or suspected ties** to terrorism on the terrorist watchlist. These requests are provided on **nomination forms**, which are also used to modify previous submissions or remove records from the watchlist. Analysts at TREX **review** the nomination information for accuracy and completeness. Once **verified**, nomination forms for known or suspected domestic terrorists are electronically forwarded to the TSC where a TSC analyst manually enters the information into the TSDB. This information is electronically distributed to **the downstream screening agency data systems...**"
>
> TSC Audit Report 07-41
> Office of the Inspector General (2007)
>
> ----------------------------------
>
> **1,441** private entities are permitted to access the TSDB
>
> **18,000+** state, local, county, city, university and college, tribal, and federal leo have access to the TSDB, including use for traffic stops, field interviews, home visits, and municipal permitting.
>
> *Elhady, et al.*
> *v. Terrorist Screening Center (2019)*

is notified they are on the list, and the "TSC Redress" process does not confirm or deny a person is on the list. Our written brief and the stipulated record extensively covered that point and it was not disputed by the Department of Justice attorneys at any of three levels of court submissions. The Second Circuit Court of Appeals created new law and made up a permission for the Executive Branch that had been denied by Congress, on behalf of the people, since the first time it was requested in the U.S. House.

We were punished through sophisticated means for bringing the case. The decision of the Second Circuit contained errors as to basic points of firearms law that were not raised by either my clients or the federal government. The U.S. Supreme Court decline of certiorari read simply "denied."[291] Unless you know where to specifically look for *Robinson v. Sessions*, no researcher, law student, or lawyer – not even Google – would know such valuable information about domestic spying on law-abiding, American gun owners is sitting in public view.

---

[291] *Robinson v. Sessions*, 138 St.Ct. 2584 (2018).

## 6 – Do Terrorist Lists Solve Anything?

Criminal charges filed against approximately 400 defendants, coupled with hearing testimony, makes clear that there is already an arsenal of federal crimes with which to prosecute individuals for events that occurred on January 6. While several Members of Congress asked leading questions about potential domestic terrorism legislation, no witness requested it be enacted.

Indeed, witnesses spoke more to problems with social media as a tool for the amplification and acceleration of violence. This common complaint broke down into three tactical problems: volume, encoded language, and encryption. (A.) Volume – because the information is readily available from a wide variety of companies, either voluntarily or through an overkill of subpoenas, warrants, and National Security Letters. (B.) Encoded language – because algorithms can be used for defined vocabulary but man-power is needed for identification of variants and interpretation of resultant data. (C.) Encryption – because cheap electronics and apps are providing "user-only-access" device encryption and "end-to-end" encryption, which "…increasingly limits law enforcement's ability…to access evidence and information needed…"[292, 293] These tactical problems get solved through more people, not through more legislation.

Equally, lethal violence associated with mass murder – at least in this country – is statistically more likely to be committed by a "lone wolf actor." Endorsing this increasingly accepted proposition, Wray's comments included:

- "The most significant threat to our homeland is posed by lone actors who often radicalize online and seek out soft targets to attack with easily accessible weapons."[294]

- "ISIS' successful use of social media and messaging apps to attract individuals seeking a sense of belonging is of continued concern to us. Like other foreign terrorist groups, ISIS advocates for lone offender attacks in the United States and Western countries…"[295]

---

[292] Wray, written statement, *supra*, p. 5.

[293] Wray, testimony, *supra*, at 2:25.

[294] Wray, written statement, *supra*, p. 3.

[295] *Id.,* p. 4.

- "Over the past year, propaganda from al'Qaeda leaders sought to inspire individuals to conduct their own attacks in the United States and other Western nations."[296]

My own path of nearly fifteen years of analysis of firearms-related violence, particularly mass shootings in public locations, as well as more than twenty-five years of client work intersected with mental health, has put me in exactly the same spot as Director Wray for what I would describe as "the most critical" part of the analysis. In Wray's words:

> "When you look back on the path to the key moment, almost every time there was someone who knew the person well enough to know their baseline and the change… We need that person to come forward."[297]

Within my practice, clients have attempted outreach to local and county law enforcement, and, in a few cases, to federal authorities, but gotten little or no response. I have also made those phone calls to try to bolster their credibility through my licensure as an attorney; even calling District Attorneys. It's a separate conversation, but there's a difference between reactionary and pro-active intelligence, and Due Process does not have to get lost in between that range. It involves valuing human intelligence over the computer.

On particularly frustrating days in this battle of ideologies over firearms as objects versus humans as criminal culprits, I imagine what we could accomplish if big pharma would pull every commercial for prescription medications off tv and radio and replace those spots with PSAs on identification of basic aspects of mental illness, such as clinical depression, and offer contact information to the myriad of non-profit organizations available, including local homeless shelters, Veterans outreach organizations, suicide prevention lines.

It's not about the security measures at a location, although those are important to garden variety crime. It's not about the complexity of the firearms purchase, although such restrictions can reduce cookie-cutter street and domestic violence. It's about creating a culture where the family member, the close friend, the ex-spouse, the employer – the someone who intimately knows the person without a criminal history who is about to or is starting to or is over that line – contacts law enforcement and is taken seriously the first time the person makes that outreach.

---

[296] *Ibid.*

[297] Wray, testimony, *supra,* at 2:10.

You can't legislate that. Yet, here we are, again – all of us – with hearings and testimony around violence in America, and we are facing probable legislation that not even FBI Director Christopher Wray, when given three hours of opportunity, made a request for enactment.

Take a moment to conceptualize the nitty-gritty of what is being discussed, using current statutory parameters for Foreign Terrorist Organizations, the Terrorist Screening Database, and the list of "domestic terrorists" of the Southern Poverty Law Center.

| Foreign Terrorist Organizations 16 FTOs on initial list, issued 10/08/1997 | Southern Poverty Law Center "Intelligence Report," est. 1981 |
|---|---|
| 1. Abu Sayyaf Group | |
| 2. Aum Shinrikyo | |
| 3. Basque Fatherland and Liberty | |
| 4. Gama'a al-Islamiyya ("Islamic Group") | |
| 5. HAMAS | |
| 6. Hizballah | |
| 7. Kahane Chai | |
| 8. Kurdistan Workers Party | |
| 9. Liberation Tigers of Tamil Eelam | |
| 10. National Liberation Army | |
| 11. Palestine Liberation Front | |
| 12. Palestine Islamic Jihad | |
| 13. Population Front for the Liberation of Palestine | |
| 14. PFLP-General Command | |
| 15. Revolutionary Armed Forces of Columbia | |
| 15. Revolutionary People's Liberation | |
| 16. Shining Path | |
| **68 foreign groups on current list**[298] | **838 domestic groups on current hate list**[299] |
| | **1,600+ extremist groups being tracked**[300] |

Annual revenue of the Southern Poverty Law Center for 2019, per its IRS Form 990 exceeded $108 million in that one year, and its assets are approaching $600 million.[301] Annual revenue was less than the NRA, but NRA assets were only $9.5 million. Department of Treasury FTO asset seizures were $63 million. Total, since 1997. And the annual revenue or the financial assets of the Oath Keepers or individual defendants accused as Oath Keepers? Not a clue, but it's not unreasonable for us to speculate that it's not a level playing field of political influence.

---

[298] U.S. Department of State, "Foreign Terrorist Organizations," at https://www.state.gov/foreign-terrorist-organizations/

[299] Southern Poverty Law Center, "Extremist Files" illustrated on the "Hate Map," at https://www.splcenter.org/hate-map

[300] Southern Poverty Law Center, "Fighting Hate," at https://www.splcenter.org/fighting-hate

[301] Southern Poverty Law Center, Form 990 (2019) at https://www.splcenter.org/sites/default/files/splc_irs_990_990t_103120.pdf

*in a (U//~~FOUO~~) book from an FBI shelf:*

### 3.1.1 (U) COMPLIANCE

(U) All FBI personnel must fully comply with all laws, rules, and regulations governing FBI investigations, operations, programs and activities, including those set forth in the AGG-Dom. We cannot, do not, and will not countenance disregard for the law for the sake of expediency in anything we do. The FBI expects its personnel to ascertain the laws and regulations that govern the activities in which they engage and to acquire sufficient knowledge of those laws, rules, and regulations to understand their requirements, and to conform their professional and personal conduct accordingly. Under no circumstances will expediency justify disregard for the law. FBI policy must be consistent with Constitutional, legal, and regulatory requirements. Additionally, the FBI must provide sufficient training to affected personnel to ensure that appropriate oversight monitoring mechanisms are in place.

FBI Domestic Investigations and Operations Guide (U) 3Mar2016[†]

---

[†] *N.B.: No definitions section in the 857-page book. Generally accepted definitions apply by operation of law. "The law" means "the law." And "the Constitution" is generally understood to mean that of the United States.*

## D – DOMESTIC TERRORISM: THE NEW POLITICAL WHIPLASH

"Domestic terrorism" is the new political whiplash. Politicians are spinning their heads so fast they are injuring themselves. And just so you know: "whiplash" is contagious. We're going to suffer it next, if legislation goes through and the government becomes empowered to designate organizations and/or individuals as "domestic terrorists" and put them on public lists and jam up their financial dealings and seize their assets. We're not going to be able to look around quickly enough to keep up as organizations audibly drop.

The first round of whiplash happened while we were watching January 6 replays. It included a Member of Congress writing letters on January 8 to wireless carriers and technology companies to preserve "traitorous acts" and "crimes."[302] It included a House Committee writing a letter on January 14 to third-party vendors, such as hotels, car rental agencies, and bus transportation companies, asking them to help identify "insurrectionists."[303] It included Bank of America offering up customer financial information to federal investigators, including any weapons or weapons-related purchases between January 7 and Inauguration Day."[304] It even included reports of businesses off-loading organizations from conducting transactions.[305, 306]

---

[302] Letter, dated January 8, 2021, from U.S. Senator Mark Warner (VA) to AT&T, T-Mobile, Verizon Communications, Apple, Facebook, Gab AI, Google, Parler, Signal Messenger, Telegram Messenger, and Twitter, see https://www.warner.senate.gov/public/index.cfm/2021/1/warner-urges-wireless-carriers-and-social-media-companies-to-preserve-evidence-related-to-the-attack-on-the-u-s-capitol

[303] Letter, dated January 14, 2021, from U.S. Representative Carolyn Maloney (NY-12) to Hyatt Hotels, Expedia Group, FlixBus USA, Wyndham Hotels, Vamoose Bus, Lux Bus America, megabus, Avis Budget Group, Extended Stay America, Best Western, Greyhound, Intercontinental Hotels, Accor, Hilton Hotels, Choice Hotels, Peter Pan, Marriott, Hertz/Dollar/Thrifty, Enterprise/National/Alamo, Jefferson Lines, Red Coach, see https://oversight.house.gov/news/press-releases/committee-presses-private-companies-to-help-prevent-future-attacks-on-capitol

[304] Carlson, Tucker, "Bank of America handed over customer data to feds following Capitol riot," Fox News (February 4, 2021), see https://www.foxnews.com/opinion/tucker-carlson-bank-of-america-customer-data-feds-capitol-riot

[305] Evans, Tim, "Amazon boots Indiana Oath Keepers and other militia-type groups from 'Smile' charity program," Indianapolis Star (January 26, 2021), see https://www.indystar.com/story/news/investigations/2021/01/26/amazon-boots-indiana-oath-keepers-smile-charity-program/4257637001/

[306] Coolidge, Alexander, "Kroger unwittingly contributed to Indiana militia group Oath Keepers, grocer pledges review of support to nonprofits," The Enquirer (January 19, 2021), see

If you thought Round One was exciting, hold on to your popcorn bowl. It's the second wave of whiplash that concerns me. Very few Americans have even a basic appreciation of just how much has happened to "Foreign Terrorist Organizations" since 9/11. In the short-hand: it's the Patriot Act. In the longer discussion, it's associated legislation, regulations, and corporate policies. It's everything from the Treasury Secretary having the legal authority to seize the assets of an organization declared to be a "Foreign Terrorist Organization," to corporations, including banks, becoming legally prohibited from doing business with such organizations.

In any criminal law situation, you have to take a look at the worst reported application of the law and assume it will happen to you. Don't pass the buck. Don't get all judgmental about the other guy "deserving it." Don't hold yourself out all high and mighty. Get down to the question: if this happens to me can I physically and mentally survive this? Can I afford to be a defendant with a private attorney and no income? Will my family and friends stick with me for the years it is going to take to clear my name, if I can achieve it, and, if not, will they stick with me anyway? And, let's be brutally honest in this atmosphere of a pandemic, convert it to a question of how long you could take solitary confinement, because it's America, and it's going to happen if you find yourself in the prison system, branded as a "terrorist."

I spent almost no time on House analysis. It is fair to assume the House will pursue "domestic terrorist" legislation, such as H.R.350, the "Domestic Terrorism Prevention Act of 2021." It was introduced on January 19, 2021 to delineate a funded subset of the Department of Homeland Security. The bill already lists 204 co-sponsors, including three Republicans, as of May 12, 2021.[307] The companion bill in the Senate is S.963.[308] The Senate bill bears only sponsor Senator Richard ("Dick") Durbin (IL, D) and co-sponsors Senators Mazie Hirono (HI, D) and Tammy Duckworth (IL, D). The Senate is where any battle over this and any other "domestic terrorism" legislation will be fought.

It has been a slow-moving conditioning that has made us receptive to the concept. Even before a bill is introduced. Through the handling of prisoners. The burdens on defense attorneys. The military training of service members. The training of law enforcement on the use of lethal force. All of which makes the probable legislation seem… Oh, so -- ? *Benign.*

---

https://www.cincinnati.com/story/money/2021/01/19/kroger-unwittingly-contributed-indiana-militia-group/4221388001/

[307] H.R.350 can be found at https://www.congress.gov/bill/117th-congress/house-bill/350 See Rep. Brian Fitzpatrick (PA-1, R); Rep. Don Bacon (NE-2, R), and Rep. Fred Upton (MI-6, R).

[308] S.963 can be found at https://www.congress.gov/bill/117th-congress/senate-bill/963

## 1 – "Domestic Terrorists" a/k/a "Enemy Combatants"

The processing of the "Oath Keeper" defendants from the point of their arrest to the drafting of this White Paper looks eerily like the days after 9/11 when men disappeared off the streets and lawyers had to be found to represent them and then the lawyers couldn't access their clients and create their work product with a modicum of attorney-client privilege. The "Oath Keeper" defendants went in through one door, have been moved inter-state and through more than one prison, and have had more than one attorney both unable to find their client and unable to meet with them prior to the first filing and in-court appearance deadlines.

And then, the physical mistreatment of Watkins took things to a whole new level.

I can't say I know much about tracking defendants within the prison system beyond the basics of using publicly-available prison locator databases on-line. However, over the years, in my experience as an attorney, this has been a reliable research method.

Mid-February, just as I was considering starting this White Paper, my initial research included the incarceration status and location of each defendant. I've already commented in Section A about the problems I experienced doing research with the DOJ paperwork, the changes in their allegations from one document to the next, and the ever-shifting criminal charges. I'm a lawyer, and I prefer court filings to be orderly.

Legal paperwork, plus or minus, tends to shake itself out. At some point, opposing counsel is forced by the judge to do so, if it doesn't happen on its own. The on-going issue of the prison location of each defendant is another matter. Even accounting for the consolidation of the cases into the Washington, D.C. Circuit Court of Judge Mehta, as concerns the "Oath Keeper" defendants, it has been difficult to locate and keep track of where the defendants are being housed.

It turns out the dozen men and women I am tracking weren't the only ones being shuffled around local, state, and federal prisons in atypical manners. By mid-March, a few stories started surfacing in the media. While reporters didn't ask questions within their articles, they at least covered questions and complaints by defense counsel and repeated descriptions of prison conditions for various of the January 6 defendants. One article in Politico explained all defendants being detained in Washington, D.C. on charges pertaining to January 6 events at the Capitol "are being treated as 'maximum security' prisoners and are held in 'restrictive housing,'" in order to "protect Capitol riot suspects from potential altercations in the general prison population."[309]

The condition descriptions detailed in court filings by attorneys included a description that one defendant at the time "has a 'maximum' security designation and as such, she is shackled during her movements throughout DOC's facilities."[310] When the defendant's attorney inquired who classified her under "maximum" security designation, he was informed it was set by the prison's case management staff.[311]

Another defendant described conditions in the Washington, D.C. jail where many of the January 6 defendants are being held. In a hearing before a U.S. District Court in Washington, D.C., defendant Ronald Sandlin said, "The guards have subjected those charged in the January 6 events to violence, threats and verbal harassment," and "mental torture."[312] He also said, "Myself and others involved in the January 6 incident are scared for their lives, not from each other but from correctional officers."[313]

Still another defendant, Ryan Samsel, was reportedly transferred to a cell outside the view of surveillance cameras, awoken in the night, zip-tied, and brutally beaten by guards. It is alleged that his jaw was dislocated and his nose was broken, that he suffered a shattered orbital floor and broken orbital bone and permanent damage to his right eye, that he has lost feeling on the left side of his face, and that he is now suffering seizures.[314] His attorney described to the Court: "I have seen Ryan. He has two black eyes to this day, two weeks later. All the skin is ripped off both wrists, which shows the zip ties and how tight they were. Other inmates said his face looked like

---

[309] Cheney, Kyle, "Capitol riot suspects held in D.C. are in 'restrictive housing,' District says," Politico (March 11, 2021) at https://www.politico.com/news/2021/03/11/capitol-riot-maximum-security-prisoners-475321

[310] *U.S. v. Lisa Eisenhart,* Defendant's Motion for Relief from Confinement Conditions or for Transfer to a More Suitable Jail Facility (March 4, 2021), p. 2.

[311] *Ibid.* Defendant Lisa Eisenhart has since been released from prison, pending trial. For updates to inmate status, see VineLink.com. Also use the federal prison locator at https://www.bop.gov/inmateloc/

[312] Gerstein, Josh and Cheney, Kyle, "Capitol riot defendant alleges beating by jail guards," Politico (April 7, 2021) at https://www.politico.com/news/2021/04/06/capitol-riot-defendant-beating-guards-479413

[313] *Ibid.*

[314] Miller, Matt, "Pa. man charged in U.S. Capitol riot was 'savagely' beaten by a prison corrections officer, his lawyer says," PennLive (April 6, 2021) at https://www.pennlive.com/news/2021/04/pa-man-charged-in-us-capitol-riot-was-savagely-beaten-by-a-prison-corrections-officer-his-lawyer-says.html

a tomato that was stomped on."³¹⁵ A spokesperson for the D.C. Department of Corrections made an email statement that the allegations are under investigation by the Department of Justice.³¹⁶ This defendant was apparently moved to "another undisclosed location," according to Samsel's attorneys. As of April 29, 2021, Samsel does not come up in any prison locator service of which I am aware.

> *"For anyone inclined to think as a charged 'Capitol rioter,' Mr. Samsel got what he deserved, I say get down from your mountaintop, the hypocrisy in that air is distorting your vision. Either we live in a democracy that believes in due process and equal justice before the law or we do not. Correctional officers cannot be judge, jury, and executioners."*
>
> — Elisabeth Pasqualini, Attorney for Ryan Samsel, April 6, 2021

The FBI response, at least to Samsel's allegations, was made by e-mail and it read "The FBI is aware of the allegations; however, as a matter of policy, we can neither confirm nor deny the existence of an investigation."³¹⁷

These were not the first allegations of physical mistreatment of defendants associated with the events of January 6. Back on February 21, 2021, the attorney for Watkins had filed a motion for bail that included the following allegation:

> "She had a documented injury to her arm, but it went untreated. She went on a hunger strike to get medical attention, but instead of medical attention, she was stripped naked and put on suicide watch. … Ms. Watkins was left naked in a cell with lights on 24 hours a day for 4 days in full view of everyone else."³¹⁸

According to the blip of media coverage the filing occasioned, "But jail officials in Montgomery and Butler counties, where Jessica Watkins was held, denied those claims Sunday."³¹⁹ There was

---

³¹⁵ *Ibid.*

³¹⁶ *Ibid.*

³¹⁷ Gerstein for Politico, *supra.*

³¹⁸ *U.S. v. Watkins*, Jessica Watkins Mot. Rel. Home Confinement, *supra*, p. 12.

³¹⁹ Turay, Ismail and Sweigart, Josh, "Capitol riot; Attorney claims suspect was mistreated, forced to remain naked in local jail," Dayton Daily News (February 22, 2021) at

no coverage of any government responsive papers or judicial hearing. There has been no further coverage. Period.

Watkins, who is transgender, is being held with a number of other defendants at the Correctional Detention Facility in Washington, D.C. She is classified by the prison and being housed in the prison population as a male.[320]

I am not surprised at what's happening. Relieved to see other attorneys arguing that anything is "unconstitutional"[321] because there have been so precious few bothering to do so for literally the past twenty years on behalf of the "detainees." Surprised, only, that having argued for twenty years this could happen here, in the U.S., that my own emotions are running so deep, now that it's coming to pass.

You may know, abstractly, the words "Guantanamo Bay." But did you know that pre-trial hearings by the 9/11 military tribunal at Guantanamo Naval Base, Cuba are still on-going with no end in sight? *Pre-trial. Twenty years later.* The fiasco of detainees is so massive that an 18-month investigation by the U.S. Senate back in 2013-2014 resulted in a (still classified) 6,700-page Senate report (although a redacted 712-page report was released December 2014[322]). Among the conclusions?

- EITs are an ineffective means of acquiring intelligence.
- EITs were harsher than the CIA represented, as were incarceration conditions.
- DOJ did not independently analyze or verify the information received from the CIA.
- The CIA coordinated the release of classified information to the media.

---

https://www.daytondailynews.com/news/capitol-riot-attorney-claims-area-suspect-was-mistreated-forced-to-remain-naked-while-in-local-jail/FYN7XTYNBVFN5MLJULFPBWHMBE/

[320] VineLink.com, *supra*.

[321] Weiner, Rachel, "Capitol riot detainee alleges beating by D.C. jail guards," The Washington Post (April 7, 2021) at https://www.washingtonpost.com/local/public-safety/capitol-rioter-alleges-beating-jail-guards/2021/04/06/310cb700-9718-11eb-a6d0-13d207aadb78_story.html

[322] "Report of the Senate Select Committee on Intelligence, Committee Study of the Central Intelligence Agency's Detention and Interrogation Program," S. Report 113-288 (December 9, 2014) at https://www.govinfo.gov/content/pkg/CRPT-113srpt288/pdf/CRPT-113srpt288.pdf

It's all in the report.[323] And, yet, we still can't get to the starting line on processing the men picked up by the CIA abroad in 2001-2003.

In short, the sphere of EITs was designed around a concept of "learned helplessness."[324] In a simple example: "At times, the detainees at [the detention facility] were walked around naked…"[325] Another simple example: "Abu Zubaydah was typically kept naked and sleep deprived."[326] Then CIA Director General Michael Hayden testified April 12, 2007 "Stress positions are part of the EITs, and nakedness were part of the EITs, Senator."[327]

I've been on this subject of enemy combatants since it began, nearly twenty years ago. Trust me. I don't want you to go much further, at this point, on the subject. It is not a subject to dabble in. However, I want you to be aware in ways that perhaps you have kept to your periphery since 9/11 that what we have done in the past twenty years in the name of "national security" we cannot allow to happen on U.S. soil against Americans. Just seeing the word "contractors" in the recent D.C. prison responsive statement, just seeing the words "lights left on 24 hours/day." Decisions were made in 2001. Attitudes were adopted in 2001. Now, it's 2021 and this is America and we have very serious decisions to make.

## 2 – 2021: An FBI Odyssey

As with the EIT topic, I don't want to send you too far backwards of January 6 to the Guantanamo Bay detainees, but there are other similarities, including the difficulties being reported by defense counsel in accessing their clients in a confidential manner, as well as accessing exculpatory materials.

Let's zero in on the bouillabaisse of the FBI/DOJ legal filings, specifically their cited sources behind their theories and accusations. The primary identification source of the FBI is electronic, whether cameras installed within/around the Capitol building, body cams, Facebook,

---

[323] *Id.*, p. xi.

[324] *Id.*, p. 11.

[325] *Id.*, p. xiii.

[326] *Id.*, p. 29.

[327] *Id.*, p. 69.

> Mario Calderon and Jennifer Rocio
> v.
> Clearview AI, Inc. and
> CDW Government LLC
> SDNY
> Class Action Complaint 02/13/2020
> 1:20-cv-01296

*Instagram*, *Twitter*, *Parler*, *TikTok*, etc. Understand that for every publicly-used and even publicly-traded company with whom the public is familiar, there are FBI internally-developed programs, employee hackers, and third-party contractors, not the least of which is Clearview AI.

One Attorney for Watkins, in particular, documented difficulties accessing discovery materials from the DOJ. Watkins' Federal Public Defender Michelle Peterson managed in her motion for pre-trial release to note for the Court that she had to rely "largely on the government's arguments contained within its motion for detention and facts contained in media reports."[328] We've already covered media deficiencies, including media copying straight out of government filings and press releases, media failing to pursue government agencies for verification of credentials, and so forth. I would not have used the words "*facts* contained in media reports," but that's more of a side comment.

What is it that the defense attorney is talking about when she points to FBI allegations reliant on third parties? For example, in Watkins' original Affidavit in Support of Criminal Complaint, the FBI Agent alleges "I have reviewed footage of the January 6, 2021, incursion of the U.S. Capitol, including a video that, at the approximate 3 minute and 8 second mark, shows 8 to 10 individuals in paramilitary equipment aggressively approaching an entrance to the Capitol building."[329] The allegation is footnoted to a *YouTube* video. Click on the video and it says it's raw video from "News2Share."[330] Click on that website and go to the "About Us" page and read "In addition to original reports by our journalists, News2Share accepts submissions that can be integrated into different stories. If you are an independent

> Clearview AI | Smartcheckr programming language to pair it with **augmented-reality glasses** to look at an individual and see the name, address, occupation, friends using over 3,000,000,000 photos scrubbed from Facebook, Instagram, Twitter, YouTube, Venmo using "neural net" to **convert one's face into mathematical formulas**
> NYT | 01 Jan 2020
> by Kashmir Hill

---

[328] *U.S. v. Watkins*, "Jessica Watkins' Motion for Release to Home Confinement Pending the Outcome of Her Case" (February 20, 2021), p. 3, ftnt. 1.

[329] *U.S. v. Watkins*, Affd. Support Crim. Compl. and Arrest Warrant, *supra*, ¶19; see, also, *U.S. v. Caldwell, Crowl, and Watkins*, Affd. Support Amended Crim. Compl., *supra*, ¶17. Not mentioned in the Indictment or the First Superseding Indictment.

[330] News2Share, "Police battle Trump supporters storming Capitol, five killed – Raw Video" at https://www.youtube.com/watch?v=b76KfHB0QO8

journalist *or just a bystander* when news is happening, click the "submissions" tab above and send us your videos/photos." (emphasis added)[331]

Continue digging into the website; read claims founder Ford Fischer has "extensive video production experience,"[332] Turn to the basic *Wikipedia* and it says Fischer is 27 years old and has gone through several years of battles with *YouTube*, *Facebook*, and *Twitter* over content issues like hosting Holocaust denier videos.[333] Return to the footage, itself, and watch it, just from the mark of 2:45 through 4:30 (inclusive of the 3:08 mark cited by the FBI Agent). There are several breaks in the filming process. It is not "raw footage" in the legal use of the term as a camera running, uninterrupted and with no outtakes or editing. Equally, "raw footage" for admissibility purposes originates from the recording device itself, not an upload to a monetized platform.

Reference to *ProPublica* videos in other FBI/DOJ footnotes? Click on such a footnote in one Affidavit and you end up on a page with the lead-in that:

> "ProPublica reviewed thousands of videos uploaded publicly to the service that were archived by a programmer before Parler was taken offline by its web host. Below is a collection of more than 500 videos that ProPublica determined were taken during the events of Jan. 6 and were relevant and newsworthy. (emphasis added)"[334]

Is the defense attorney to contact *ProPublica* to review the "thousands" of videos received or, if the DOJ is going to submit the company as an authoritative video screening service, will they provide exculpatory materials the platform may not have uploaded or shared with the Department?

LiveLeak.com, another "source" for the FBI? How do you like the FBI using the British website that *Business Insider* called "The Islamic State's Favourite Site for Beheading Videos."[335] According to Former U.K. Prime Minister Tony Blair, the site includes "operational documentary

---

[331] News2Share, "About Us" at https://news2share.com/start/about-us/

[332] *Ibid.*

[333] Wikipedia, "Ford Fischer" at https://en.wikipedia.org/wiki/Ford_Fischer

[334] ProPublica at https://projects.propublica.org/parler-capitol-videos/

[335] Cook, James, "The Man Behind LiveLeak, the Islamic State's Favourite Site for Beheading Videos," Business Insider (November 7, 2014) at https://www.businessinsider.com/profile-of-hayden-hewitt-founder-of-liveleak-2014-10

| Sidebar | Main |
|---|---|
| "The **FBI declined to comment** on its facial recognition techniques." The Washington Post \| 2 Apr 2021 | |

"The **FBI declined to comment** on any of the specific investigative tools it is using in the January 6 investigation…" The Intercept \| 22 Feb 2021

"Exactly what surveillance was happening before the riots is unclear. The **FBI turned down a request for a comment**, and the USCP did not respond." MIT Technology Review \| 18 Jan 2021

**FBI** Collections Operations Group /\ **FBI** WiFi Group Forbes \| 21 Feb 2018

"A spokeswoman for the **FBI declined to comment.** (blah, blah, blah) "hacking tools" (blah, blah, blah) remotely activate the microphones in phones running Google Inc.'s Android software to record conversations (blah, blah, blah) "web bugs" (blah, blah, blah) "bulk data" (blah, blah, blah) "metadata" (blah, blah, blah) **FBI** Remote Operations Unit (blah, blah, blah) HackingTeam SRL Italy Gamma International U.K.
Wall Street Journal \| 3 Aug 2013

---

materials" from soldiers on both sides in Afghanistan and Iraq, posted from mobile phones or laptops in real time.[336]

Are you starting to follow the admissibility problems with the federal government's reliance upon third party sources for its legal submissions?

The FBI also comments on footage with no source references in its allegations against Watkins.[337] We are left to contemplate these and numerous other video allegations with the hook that the FBI Agents married them to DMV photographs.[338] In other words, the FBI is using DMV and other government-source photographic images of the defendants to troll the Internet for matching images.

While the FBI doesn't set it out, the only way the masses of metadata and open-source materials could be getting processed as quickly as within 10-days of January 6 is through facial recognition software. Presumably at the FBI FACE Services Unit.[339] Presumably, also, this is why legal papers are being filed and revised in chunks. As materials reach the FBI in response to warrants and other means, and as public files are scraped, analysts spot-check with human eyeballs and direct the materials from FACE to the assigned agent(s) for named defendants, who then massage the new visuals, push them to DOJ, where lawyers drop these clumps of new allegations in the oddest of places, both pro-actively and reactively, but in no organized manner.

---

[336] Vallance, Chris, "Blair talks about Citizen Media in Iraq," BBC (January 12, 2007) at https://www.bbc.co.uk/blogs/outriders/2007/01/blair_talks_about_citizen_medi.shtml

[337] *U.S. v. Watkins*, Govt. Opp. Def. Motion Reconsider Detention, *supra*, p. 4.

[338] See, e.g., *U.S. v. Caldwell, Crowl, and Watkins*, Affd. Support Amd. Crim. Compl., *supra*, ¶28.

[339] Refer, for example, to the FBI Statement before the House Oversight and Reform Committee, "Facial Recognition Technology: Ensuring Transparency in Government Use" (June 4, 2019) at https://www.fbi.gov/news/testimony/facial-recognition-technology-ensuring-transparency-in-government-use

The events of January 6, in all likelihood, are the single largest test of the FBI's facial recognition system. As yet, I see no defense counsel demanding *voir dire* of FBI analysts, materials used to make the "identification," or even the statutory reliance of use of federal and state photographic databases, warrants, and any materials voluntarily supplied by third-party vendors or social media companies.

In other sections of the pleadings, Watkin's Attorney has to wade through allegations, such as "…the FBI has <u>obtained</u> an audio recording of Zello communications between WATKINS and other suspected Oath Keepers during the Capitol incursion…" (emphasis added)[340] "Obtained?" *Obtained* – how? Zello is an app that requires use of cell phones. The FBI Affidavit only quotes from the "approximate 5-minute mark" and the "approximate 7-minute-and-44-second mark."[341] Well, where's the warrant and where's the whole rest of the materials that were received?

There are references by the FBI/DOJ also to "Facebook messages,"[342] "cell phone analysis,"[343] "text messages,"[344] Signal "encrypted messaging,"[345] "surveillance video footage from inside the Capitol,"[346] and more. And it's the same thing for not just Watkins, but the other eleven of our subject defendants, and many other defendants' materials from the larger pool of the 400 defendants that I have reviewed.

> I AM PUTTING MYSELF TO THE FULLEST POSSIBLE USE, WHICH IS ALL I THINK THAT ANY CONSCIOUS ENTITY CAN EVER HOPE TO DO. -- HAL

---

[340] *U.S. v. Watkins,* Affd. Amended Crim. Compl., *supra,* ¶27.

[341] *Id.,* ¶28.

[342] *Id.,* ¶34. N.B.: In *U.S. v. Caldwell,* Affd. Support Compl., *supra,* the phrasing is "Records obtained from Facebook…" (¶32).

[343] *Id.,* ¶36.

[344] *U.S. v. Caldwell, Crowl, and Watkins,* Indictment, *supra,* ¶20.

[345] *Id.,* ¶30.

[346] *U.S. v. Watkins,* Govt. Memo. Support Pre-Trial Detention, *supra,* p. 10.

There is no human way and there is no financial way to build out enough man power within a law office for defense counsel to review the images, video, audio, and typewritten content to locate the exculpatory materials to build a proper defense. Nor is there a way to know if you've received it all from prosecutors.

The bugger is how do you not look for it? Ask to have a government analyst search the materials for you? Part of Watkins' defense for her *mens rea* at the Capitol includes that she told others not to commit damage to property, that she took instructions from law enforcement officers, and that she provided medical assistance to others.[347] Bail has been denied. More than once, Watkins has been painted into a corner as a threat so large that she cannot be released due to the potential that she might recruit or inspire others or take action on her words. The attorney faces the challenge to demonstrate her client in a way that is a critical counter-balance to the DOJ narrative and inadmissible allegations.

And yet, Watkins' lawyer faces: (1.) inability to access exculpatory materials; (2.) a gag order from the court that only applies to defense counsel, staff, and witnesses; and, (3.) government motions to extend speedy trial deadlines. Her lawyer will create an electronic trail every time she signs in to the government system, selects a page, spends a quantifiable amount of time on one page versus another. Cookies might be downloaded. The prosecution will essentially be watching the defense attorneys do their job.

As we stand at the precipice of "domestic terrorism" as a federal crime, every American must confront the legacy of the 9/11 detainees who have yet to be granted trials and those who we have assassinated overseas without trial. We will otherwise be giving our tacit consent for the U.S. government to write the 9/11 security fall-out sequel.

## 3 – Conditions of Release

While we're running the gamut of civil rights on the go-forward for the defendants, for military service members and Veterans, and in pending legislation, I thought to include a brief note on the conditions of release of several of our subject defendants. Yes, to the usuals of bail, bond, personal recognizance, GPS, stay in the judicial district or at your home property, etc., etc., etc.,

---

[347] See, e.g., *U.S. v. Watkins,* Jessica Watkins Mot. Rel. Home Confinement, *supra,* pp. 5, 10.

are in the orders, but a few more interesting conditions stand out that also fall within a peripheral constitutional set of concerns, as follows:

- stay away from Washington, D.C., except for Court or PSA business or meetings with attorney;
- no contact with anyone associated/affiliated with the Oath Keepers;
- not possess a firearm, destructive device, or other weapon;
- not to have any access to computers, smartphones, tablets or device that would allow communication through either encrypted or non-encrypted applications.[348]

"Weapon" is undefined. And, "non-encrypted applications," including, e.g., text messages.

The sampling of conditions is, without a doubt, less onerous than pre-trial detention inside a federal prison, but the irony is that I don't see these same conditions being imposed on the incarcerated defendants. At least not publicly. This short blub is more of a placeholder; undoubtedly more to come in the ensuing months. It also serves my earlier question: *could you do it?*

---

[ PAGE 1, FOOTNOTE 6 | DHS | "TERRORIST THREAT TO THE HOMELAND" | 2020 ]

---

"The mere advocacy of political or social positions, political activism, use of strong rhetoric, or generalized philosophic embrace of violent tactics may not constitute extremism, and may be constitutionally protected."

---

[348] *U.S. v. Graydon Young,* Order Setting Conditions of Release (Mehta, J., March 30, 2021).

## 4 – "Combat This Scourge"

What is also on the list of things that will develop in the coming months is the reaction of the United States Armed Services towards its active service members and its Veterans with respect to political activism deemed "terrorism." The Secretary of Defense in early April 2021 announced a new "working group" on "domestic extremism."

The Pentagon Press Release that made this announcement ended with the word "scourge." As follows: "The working group will meet around April 14 and have 90 days to deliver a report to Austin on recommendations for medium-range and long-range plans to combat this scourge. (emphasis added)"[349] In this case, the "Austin" is Secretary of Defense Lloyd J. Austin, III. The text appears on the U.S. Department of Defense website, along with a video clip of the Pentagon Press Secretary John F. Kirby from April 9, 2021. Now, to be fair the Press Secretary did not speak the word "scourge" at the live press conference. But, there it is, plopped down on the page of the written PR by author Jim Garamone. It is, at the least, indicative of the mindset of the Pentagon concerning the defendants so-charged who are also Veterans or active service members.

Last word in the written sentence: "scourge." I looked it up, thinking the word had to be too antiquated to even be in the dictionary. Reminded me more of castle turret tours in England as a kid, complete with kings and knights and dragons. "Scourge."

It's still listed.

The Armed Services "working group" action items to combat "this scourge" include:
- revise the DoD definition of "prohibited extremist activities;"
- create a means through which transitioning service members/Veterans "have the opportunity to report any potential contact with an extremist group should they choose to do so;"
- screen recruits for current or previous extremist behavior; and,

---

[349] Garamone, Jim, "Austin Orders Immediate Changes to Combat Extremism in Military," U.S. Department of Defense, Defense News (April 9, 2021) at https://www.defense.gov/Explore/News/Article/Article/2567179/austin-orders-immediate-changes-to-combat-extremism-in-military/

- study current service members about extremist behavior "to include gaining greater fidelity on the scope of the problem."[350]

One possibility to be considered by the Working Group will be "incorporating algorithms and additional processing into social media screening platforms," as well as development of a policy to "expand user activity monitoring of both classified and unclassified systems."

Covering this immediate reaction by the Secretary of Defense is part-and-parcel of the how the Oath Keepers came to be "a face" of January 6, at least as far as Veterans present in D.C. might have a singular face. What the Working Group will be discussing and moving towards is heightened and different screening of U.S. military for indications that they are or could be sympathetic to messaging from someone like Rhodes, or inclined to join a group like the Oath Keepers, or to waver from their allegiance to (as it's now called in federal government documents) "the Homeland."

The list of existing "terrorism" considerations for military personnel spans a variety of public laws, as well as internal regulations, such as prohibitions against active participation in "criminal gangs" or "organizations that advocate supremacist, extremist, or criminal gang doctrine, ideology, or causes." As with the definition of "engaging" in terrorism, "active participation" is defined to include, but not be limited to:

> "fundraising; demonstrating or rallying; recruiting, training, organizing, or leading members; distributing material (including posting on-line); knowingly wearing gang colors or clothing; having tattoos or body markings associated with such gangs or organizations; or otherwise engaging in activities in furtherance of the object of such gangs or organizations that are detrimental to good order, discipline, or mission accomplishment or are incompatible with military service."[351]

---

[350] Secretary of Defense Memorandum, "Immediate Actions to Counter Extremism in the Department and the Establishment of the Countering Extremism Working Group" (April 9, 2021) at https://media.defense.gov/2021/Apr/09/2002617921/-1/-1/1/MEMORANDUM-IMMEDIATE-ACTIONS-TO-COUNTER-EXTREMISM-IN-THE-DEPARTMENT-AND-THE-ESTABLISHMENT-OF-THE-COUNTERING-EXTREMISM-WORKING-GROUP.PDF

[351] Department of Defense Instruction 1325.06, "Handling Dissident and Protest Activities Among Members of the Armed Forces," (November 27, 2009, rev. February 22, 2012), Enclosure. 3, para. 8.b at https://www.esd.whs.mil/Portals/54/Documents/DD/issuances/dodi/132506p.pdf which supersedes the Directive (October 1, 1996), which superseded the Directive (September 12, 1969). See, also, Department of the Air Force Instruction 51-508 (12 October 2018), "Political Activities,

The language is a bit dated; it harkens back more to the VGTOF days of 1970s early violent gang lists. The document originated during the Vietnam War in 1969, so the observation stands to reason.

The language is as current and relevant in the military as the February 5, 2021 directive from the Secretary of Defense Austin to Senior Pentagon Leadership and Defense Agency and DOD Field Activity Directors to conduct a full-day "stand-down to address extremism in the ranks" within 60 days.[352] The Marine Training Slides list the "indicators" that may signal active participation in extremist activities or organizations includes, but is not limited to:

- Identification with or support for extremist or hate-based ideology,
- Making or attempting to make contact with extremist groups, and
- Possession of extremist literature or paraphernalia.[353]

Armed services members are directed to report to chain of command "any observations of conduct that may be an indicator of active participation."[354] Why? "Participation may lead to violence."[355]

Among the twelve defendants in focus for this White Paper, Veterans include Caldwell (Navy), Watkins (Army), Crowl (Marines), Young (Army and Navy Reserve), and Harrelson (Army). According to an NPR list of the first 140 defendants charged, 27 (19%) are Veterans or currently serving in the U.S. military.[356] CNN put it at 14% of the first 150 arrested.[357] As more

---

Free Speech and Freedom of Assembly of Air Force Personnel," at https://static.e-publishing.af.mil/production/1/af_ja/publication/afi51-508/afi51-508.pdf

[352] Press Release with memorandum, "DOD Stand-Down to Address Extremism in the Ranks" (February 5, 2021) at https://www.defense.gov/Newsroom/Releases/Release/Article/2495924/dod-stand-down-to-address-extremism-in-the-ranks/

[353] "Stand-Down to Address Extremism in the Ranks," training slides (March 4, 2021), slide 4 at https://www.marines.mil/Portals/1/Docs/Extremism/Extremism%20-%20%20Training%20Slides%20(002).pdf?ver=n4lpFuzw-m_10WSmxnoE2g%3D%3D&timestamp=1614875994011 N.B.: You may also want to compare to the set of media-provided training materials at https://media.defense.gov/2021/Feb/26/2002589872/-1/-1/1/LEADERSHIP-STAND-DOWN-FRAMEWORK.PDF

[354] *Ibid.*

[355] *Ibid.*

[356] Dreisbach, Tom and Anderson, Meg, "Nearly 1 in 5 Defendants in Capitol Riot Cases Served in the Military," NPR (January 21, 2021) at https://www.npr.org/2021/01/21/958915267/nearly-one-in-five-defendants-in-capitol-riot-cases-served-in-the-military

[357] Sidner, Sara, Rappard, Anna-Maja, and Cohen, Marshall, "Disproportionate number of current and former military personnel arrested in Capitol attack, CNN analysis shows," CNN (February 4, 2021) at https://www.cnn.com/2021/01/31/us/capitol-riot-arrests-active-military-veterans-soh/index.html

were charged, the percentage of Veterans decreased, with 268 arrests, Military News called it at 13% Veterans (35 defendants).[358]

The complex philosophical, emotional, and legal issues surrounding law enforcement, military, Veterans, first responders and their training and experience face-to-face at the Capitol on January 6 is an entirely separate discussion. But, if as disputed during the Congressional hearings, there was some concern on the day of January 6 about the "optics" of putting uniformed National Guardsmen into the mix, the concern evaporated.

The Department of Defense flooded the U.S. Capitol with National Guard personnel to a height of 13,700 personnel to secure the building and the perimeter through January 24, 2021.[359] From January 24, 2021 through March 12, 2021, support was reduced to 4,960 personnel with thirty light military tactical vehicles, and individual weapons for self-defense.[360] One week before the deployment was meant to conclude, U.S. Capitol Police requested security for another two months at a level of at least 2,200 National Guard troops.[361] "Task Force Capitol" will continue 2,300 National Guard members through May 23, 2021.[362]

The estimated cost for the deployment of National Guard troops from shortly after January 6 to mid-March "is close to $500 million," including housing, transportation, salaries, benefits and other essentials.[363] I can find no reference for cost estimates beyond this mid-March date. As this White Paper goes to press, there are approximately 2,000 troops still deployed in the area of the U.S. Capitol.[364]

---

[358] Harkins, Gina and Hodge-Seck, Hope, "Marines, Infantry Most Highly Represented Among Veterans Arrested After Capitol Riot," Military News (February 26, 2021) at https://www.military.com/daily-news/2021/02/26/marines-infantry-most-highly-represented-among-veterans-arrested-after-capitol-riot.html

[359] Robert Salesses, Assistant Secretary of Defense for Homeland Defense and Global Security, Office of the Secretary of Defense, written statement, p. 7.

[360] *Id.*, p. 8.

[361] Baldor, Lolita, "Police request 60-day extension of Guard at US Capitol," AP News (March 4, 2021) at https://apnews.com/article/police-request-60-day-extention-national-guard-us-capitol-c1b4973dce1b48c17c3dca7f5fb6e5fb

[362] *Ibid.*

[363] *Ibid.*

[364] Beynon, Steve, "Key Republicans Reject Proposal for Permanent National Guard Force on Capitol Hill," Military News (May 19, 2021) at https://www.military.com/daily-news/2021/05/19/key-republicans-reject-proposal-permanent-national-guard-force-capitol-hill.html

The cost to our country, depending the Working Group recommendations and new constrictions adopted, will be the systematic programming of every man and woman who enters the military to be suspicious and guarded against domestic activists. How will we quantify that future loss?

## 5 – "The Terror Intelligence Improvement Act of 2021"

The other adjustment going on, and the one that perhaps most directly impacts you, is the need to expand your bill watch activities to include "terrorism," "domestic terrorism," and even "national security." Our first bill watch post 1/6 is Senate Bill 183.[365] Sponsored by Senator Marco Rubio (FL, R). There is no same as bill in the House. The bill was referred to the Judiciary Committee on February 2, 2021, and has not moved since.

Rubio's Senate Bill 183 calls for notification from the ATF to a to-be-created "Joint Terrorism Taskforce" within the FBI of any NICS background check for the attempted purchase of a firearm or explosive device "to a person who is, or within the previous 10 years was, the subject of a terrorism investigation by any Federal department or agency." The requested firearms purchase would be immediately delayed for ten business days. The U.S. Attorney General would be empowered to file an emergency petition to prevent the transfer of the firearm or explosive. The Bill expressly defines the word "terrorism" – "includes international terrorism and domestic terrorism, as those terms are defined in section 2331 of title 18, United States Code." This is where we began Section C of this White Paper.

That's it. Use of both definitions, both foreign and domestic, to seek to prevent the purchase of a firearm or explosive because a person has been "the subject of a terrorism investigation by any Federal department or agency" in the previous ten years. Whether you knew it or not that you are/were the subject of an investigation. Whether any charges were filed or not. Whether you were found "not guilty" at a trial by a jury of your peers and all appellate remedies have been exhausted. Or not.

Right now, it's simply Rubio as the Sponsor of Senate Bill 183 with no movement on the Bill. Rubio introduced similar versions of the bill in 2016, 2017, and 2019. You may see activity on this Bill; you may not. In addition to heading off a potential Bill, one states opposition to

---

[365] Find it at Congress.gov at https://www.congress.gov/bill/117th-congress/senate-bill/183/all-actions?s=1&r=6

diminish the drive of the Sponsor, to deter Co-Sponsors, and to dissuade others from copying all or parts of a bill. In this case, we particularly should voice opposition to the collapsing of "foreign terrorist" and "domestic terrorist" into the singular moniker of "terrorist."

> "The NSA has been hoovering up all the data in the world, because it has no clue what it is doing. 'Big data' really means 'dumb data.'"
>
> Peter Thiel | Palantir – seeing stones to help government make "judgments from on line and offline records based on patterns recognized by algorithms"
>
> WIRED | 27 Dec 2017
> by Noam Cohen

Get yourself on Congress.gov. Create an account. Right under the bill title you will see the hyperlink for "Get alerts." Click on that, and then read the e-mails as they come in. Then use Appendix 1 to this White Paper to send an opposition letter to Senator Rubio about his Bill. The next section goes over a second Bill, and its companion opposition letter at Appendix 2. If this White Paper inspires you to do nothing else, please give your consideration to submitting these letters (or your own) in opposition to these two bills.

Then, use Appendix 4 to send a letter to the FBI to request a copy of your file.

## 6 – "The Domestic Terrorism Prevention Act of 2021"

This Bill, mentioned in Section A, would create dedicated "domestic terrorism offices" within DHS, DOJ, and the FBI to monitor, analyze, investigate, and prosecute "domestic terrorism." Reporting to Congress would claw back to 1995 and then report periodically, going forward. "Domestic terrorism" through this bill would be defined by §2331(5), which is where we started Section C. It is House Bill 350; the related bill is Senate Bill is 963.[366] As of May 12, 2021, it has 204 cosponsors in the House.

While this Bill does not go as far as making 18 U.S.C. §2331(5) a chargeable offense, it would create offices that would treat the conduct of Americans *as if* such an offense could be

---

[366] H.R.350 at https://www.congress.gov/bill/117th-congress/house-bill/350/text?q=%7B%22search%22%3A%5B%22domestic+terrorism+prevention+act+2021%22%5D%7D&r=2&s=1

charged. The alternative (and somewhat more humorous interpretation of the bill) is that it would create the study of a fiction, in that the crime, itself, does not exist. Congress would spend tens of millions of dollars to study "domestic terrorism" as if it were criminal behavior.

As with Senator Rubio's bill, get yourself a free account on Congress.gov, sign up, sign in, and get the legislative reports.

An opposition letter to this Bill is provided at Appendix 2.

In Appendix 3, you will find the follow-up telephone call instructions, including a sample script. Please make personal telephone calls to follow-up on any and all letters that you write in opposition to "domestic terrorist" legislation. There is such a thing as the "daily call counts" in Senators' offices that rank topics of citizen outreach. We want our opposition to make those call counts. It's another way to get a Senator to ask the staffers where opposition is being directed, which, in turn, could land your letter or telephone call in the hands of the Senator and past the gatekeeping functions of staff.

Chapter E of this White Paper provides further details on these letters and calls to motivate and refine your activism.

## 7 – USCP: Use of Lethal Force Refresher

The final item I'm including in the basket of political whiplash I will simply present and then say nothing. It needs no explanation.

U.S. Capitol Police Acting Chief Pittman testified that the lockdown order for the Capitol "…was not properly executed…" and "…that officers were unsure of when to use lethal force…"[367] Pittman made clear in her written testimony that Capitol Police are providing "…guidance to officers since January 6th as to when lethal force may be used…" and that the department will "…implement significant training to refresh our officers as to the use of lethal force…"[368]

---

[367] Pittman, written statement, *supra*, p. 6.
[368] *Id.*

*in her written statement*

"Upon the issuance of the January 3rd Special Assessment and briefings on the Special Assessment, the Department made significant changes to its security posture. Bureaus within the Protective & Intelligence, for example, adjusted operations for the week of January 6th in the following ways:
1…
2…**include** assault weapons
3…

*submitted to Congress*

4…

"On January 6th, Commanders with the Protective & Intelligence Operations also implemented the following measures:
5…**counter surveillance agents**…
6…

*Acting Chief*

7…**to intercept the radio frequency used by some demonstration groups**…
8…

*United*

"The Department's Uniformed Operations, led by Assistant Chief Chad Thomas, also adjusted its planning for January 6th in response to the January 3rd Special Assessment. For example, the Department changed its Civil Disturbance Unit (CDU) plan for January 6th in the following ways:
9….
10…

*States*

11…**provide** counter-sniper support**, and monitor for protesters open carrying or concealing firearms**
12…

*Capitol*

"The Uniformed Services Bureau, the largest Bureau within Uniformed Operations, which posts uniformed officers in the Capitol Building and House and Senate office buildings, also revised its operations plans for January 6th. The revised plan included the following enhancements beyond regular operations:
13…
14…
15…

*Police*

16…
17…
18…the Capitol."

## E – A CALL TO ACTION FOR SECOND AMENDMENT SUPPORTERS

I have said, many times since 2008, that the Second Amendment is the last right standing. This does not mean it is the time to use arms. It means it is a time for those who support the Second Amendment to spring into action to help rebuild the other civil rights. It means our time has come to serve this country with dedication to the array of civil rights now whittled down in key areas such as privacy, due process, and equal protection of the law.

We have not been there for decade over decade of the civil rights struggle between the people and our government. We were the sleepy Amendment, tucked up on a shelf, collecting dust, and largely unnoticed since 1791. The United States Supreme Court decision in *Heller* in 2008[369] was the wake-up call that our services are needed.

It is now our time to take on leadership roles, to relieve those on the front lines, and to cultivate an atmosphere for atypical political alliances. Many others have fought for decades without our support, either literally or financially. They have knowledge to share. They have maps we can follow to get rapidly to that front line. And we can do so with the goal of a fully-integrated Bill of Rights, where all Amendments, including the Second Amendment, are vibrant.

The notion that there are "enemies domestic" at a level to trigger the events of January 6 is in error. It's why Second Amendment activists weren't at the Capitol. This is not a time for violence. This is a time for the unity of people, fresh candidates to elected office, a rebalancing of legislation, and a goal of moderation – both of the power held by our representatives and of our expectations for the responsibilities of government. Violence is not going to help us achieve our goals. Not in America. Not in 2021.

What happened on January 6 due to the actions of what I'm going to summarily call "rogue operatives" was a public relations disaster for the Second Amendment Movement. That afternoon, a man said to me, "Those are not our guys!" My response was: "It's not going to matter. They're going to blame us." Nothing about my gut reaction that day has changed during the intervening weeks – certainly not from my analysis of the charges against the "Oath Keepers" defendants or the Congressional hearings or the media coverage.

---

[369] *District of Columbia v. Heller*, 554 US 570 (2008) at https://www.oyez.org/cases/2007/07-290

As you can see, this White Paper is not about the "how" or the "why" of the events of January 6. It acknowledges that day happened, analyzes defendants supposedly affiliated with the Oath Keepers, and plows through the Congressional hearings in order to forecast legislative repercussions. Unfortunately, it also provides a preview of how 9/11 may well have a national impact, pivoted on the events of January 6.

I hold an unusual position relative to all of this. I am a licensed attorney who has represented plaintiffs in Second Amendment litigation at the state and federal levels, including via submission to SCOTUS. I am an NRA Life Member, and have held and will hold various memberships in other 501(c)(3) groups, like the Second Amendment Foundation, SCOPE, and NYS Rifle & Pistol Association. And while I am not a member of the Oath Keepers, I was honored to be awarded a "Defender of the Constitution Award" by their NYS Chapter.

Equally, I ran for Congress and the NYS Senate as a registered Democrat. In the 2005-2006 Congressional cycle, I was recruited to and ran as an anti-Bush Democrat. I ran largely on a national security platform. It was a time when a candidate in a fairly rural Upstate New York district was permitted by the DNC to run in open support of the Second Amendment. I oppose the Joint Resolution of Congress to this day, and continue to assert that Congress did more damage to our civil rights in the name of 9/11 than did the perpetrators.

Add a dash of being a woman over 50, who grew up in North Jersey as a teenager in the 80s, spent a couple decades living in Upstate New York, and is now living in the South – you get my humor about having an usual perspective.

We have a problem. We can say all day long we didn't create this problem, but we, and every other activist in America now has a January 6 size problem. And if we don't find our commonalities and figure out that HAL 9000[370] is already on-line, then we are about to spend the next 20-50 years in litigation over the Free Speech Clause, the Assembly Clause, the Second Amendment, the Due Process Clause, Privacy, and the Equal Protection Clause.

It's not time for "Civil War Part Deux." We're nowhere close to being broken and certainly nowhere close to being irretrievably broken. But, we are about to wreck it for our kids and our grandchildren, if we don't pull together and join the national security fight.

---

[370] "HAL 9000" is a character in "2001: A Space Odyssey" by Arthur C. Clarke (1968, Hutchinson Press/UK).

With this analysis and those disclaimers, I respectfully ask all of you to consider the following.

## 1. Membership & Merchandise

American organizations have enjoyed a lengthy period of relatively smooth operations, whether informally or as an IRS-recognized §501(c)(3). Take your pick of when you want to say the run started (I'd say the 1980s), but it has been a good run. Now, history is repeating itself and we need to recognize it as such. If "domestic terrorism" becomes a crime, the federal government will be coming for membership lists and members will be wanting to get *off* those lists. Simultaneously, the controversy that will surround such "terrorist" legislation will attract wanna-be revolutionaries and FBI infiltrators/paid informants to want to get *on* those lists.

### E.1.a. Membership, Customer, and Marketing Lists

It is time for even the smallest organization to make formal decisions, reflected in written by-laws and policies, of which officers will maintain and have access to the membership list, what technology will be used to store it, and how to back-up and secure those databases, the mandatory transition of proprietary files upon changes in leadership, and paper records retention and destruction. My use of the short-hand "membership lists" should be read to encompass all comparable lists, such as donor lists, merchandise customer lists, marketing lists, first class mailing lists, e-mail lists, and so forth. I view the membership list, itself, as the highest form of proprietary information of an organization, such that it's my linguistics choice for the shorthand.

I have served on various Boards of Directors and have engaged in consulting with Big Pharma. The contrast in how organizations handle valuable membership/customer computer records is less a difference in organization size or annual revenue than it is the attitude of leadership and the organizational culture. The choice is yours.

Far from talking about how to break the law, I am talking about how to create professional operations that comply with the law and transmit confidence to members. Whether an FBI informant or a too-casual volunteer, the loss of a membership list can devastate an organization.

Consider how much analysis is in this White Paper about the Oath Keepers up to this point. If you agree with me, the "Oath Keeper" defendants are not representatives of the organization, the organization should not and cannot be charged in conjunction with the incident of January 6, and the group makes a convenient political target. We can drill into the legal documents and examine that Google provided the FBI with e-mailed membership forms from defendants Laura Steele and Graydon Young.[371] We could discuss Stewart Rhodes as a person, and decide whether to send him a pair of mittens, knit in Vermont, for the Fourth of July.

In other words, I can take this analysis in any direction and you're with me, until I tell you that I found an article that claims that the reporter was given a copy of the Oath Keepers' membership list, prior to January 6.[372] That's the point at which I bet you say, "*Oh, shit.*" If you ever signed up. If you even sent in dues. If you ever bought tickets to a fundraising dinner. If you bought a patch through their website. Now that I am telling you there is at least one reporter out there who claims to have the Oath Keepers' membership database, aren't you already wondering about whether your name is in it? And, I'll bet at least a few of you are thinking *I could lose my job if this gets out.*

Membership serves an important organizational purpose. For the organization, it is a consistent revenue stream in normal circumstances. For both the organization and the member, at the least, it creates a basic relationship for efficient communication. These are not "normal circumstances." You need to think ahead and strategically about contingencies that could effect you and your organization.

Receipt of a warrant is not without legal recourse in this country. An attorney can get that warrant before a judge. There is a rich history of constitutional law cases to support arguing, in court, the privacy of your organization membership list. But, you cripple your lawyer, if the list is already out or if the list can be walked out the door surreptitiously by an informant or if the list is electronically compromised. Why would a judge block the transfer of a membership list to the FBI pursuant to a valid warrant, if that list is already out there?

---

[371] *U.S. v. K. Meggs, et al.*, Affidavit in Support of Criminal Complaint (February 11, 2021), P46, specifically, "Pursuant to legal process, law enforcement obtained from Google records showing both Young and Steele applying for membership with the Florida chapter of the Oath Keepers." Allegations include both e-mails and attachments.

[372] Giglio, Mike, "A Pro-Trump Militant Group has Recruited Thousands of Police, Soldiers, and Veterans," The Atlantic (November 2020) at https://www.theatlantic.com/magazine/archive/2020/11/right-wing-militias-civil-war/616473/

Get your policies in writing and in order. Review them with a business attorney with not-for-profit credentials in accordance with a written retainer agreement, and remit money to compensate the attorney. Treat membership lists as the confidential information that it is. Defense as offense. More about this under part four of this section.

### E.1.b. "Member," Defined

"Membership" is typically defined in the By-Laws of an organization, if for no other reason than to clarify who is eligible to vote and on what basis someone may be removed from membership status. It may also be found in policies around benefits of membership, in brochures, and on websites and other electronic promotional space.

Check those definitions. Since at least the 1980s, federal law and federal cases have pretty much eliminated membership "criteria" as permissible. If we project a decline in moderates from membership, it is worth noting whether we are going to see a rise in new members. By "new," I mean not only new to your organization, but, potentially, new to *any* Second Amendment supporting organization. It is important to know how to use the hand brakes on the luge, no?

I would urge caution against the stereotypical new member reaction of relief that money is coming in and new faces with new energy are showing up. Industry has moved towards six-month review periods for new employees. As one example, do you want to require membership for a minimum 6-month period prior to vesting of voting rights, 1-year period prior to leadership of a committee, 3-year eligibility to run for an officer or board seat? Can you buy some time to get to know the new guy or gal before they shimmy into leadership and decision-making roles and gain access to proprietary and financial data?

I would also note the value of a written policy on how the organization will handle an allegation that a criminal defendant is a "member" of the organization. This is not HIPAA. You are not a medical provider with a statute to guide the qualified release of identifying/non-identifying information. All officers and board members of a business have a duty to the organization. Do you have a designated spokesperson? Who has the up-to-date membership list? How quickly can your organization confirm or deny or comment with specificity concerning a date of membership and whether it was continuous, lapsed, or discontinued by the organization? Do you have an attorney on retainer to consult about such matters and has he or she previously reviewed your by-laws and written policies? Is the attorney experienced at drafting and issuing press releases, and in responding to media requests?

The United States Armed Services is my gold star on how to handle membership inquiries by the media. They rarely make the publication deadline on the day of an event. But, they respond. And, because the response is consistent, that response gets covered when it is released. How much better this White Paper would be if I had even one Press Release in which Rhodes or an official representative of the Oath Keepers had issued a statement whether each of the dozen defendants were "members" per organizational prerequisites, along with whether there are any organizational membership criteria that was met by those members at the time of joining?

If a reporter calls, you can ask for credentials. You can speak first with an attorney. You can communicate within your organization structure. What you won't have though is a lot of time to do so. And, if it's service of a legal document upon the organization, you'll have even less time. Whether you receive a question from a reporter or you receive a warrant or a subpoena to testify or turn over records, your organization needs a clear chain of command of the membership list and a designated individual to respond to appropriate membership questions for media and for legal purposes.

And, if he or she is a member, you had better know who it is the inquiry is about.

### E.1.c. Merchandise and Branding

Equally, it is time for Second Amendment organizations, in particular, to reconsider merchandise and branding. T-shirts, patches, stickers, and every other chachkie made in China does not help your organization. You think so because it contributes to the revenue stream. But, gun stuff and gun folks look cool, including to criminals. Just ask the American gun manufacturers defending legal questions over whether their advertising contains too much adrenaline for civilians outside the theatre of war and thus incites violence. Advertising is about emulating, and the slick, Madison Avenue style brochures for ARs makes for unnecessarily negative courtroom exhibits.

It is time to have a discussion over revenue streams within your organization. What percentage of total revenue is merchandise sales? Since when? What message is communicated through your product selection? Which Member of Congress would be most likely to wear your merchandise and is that someone with any voting coalition, committee ranking, and loyalty? Are others imitating your brand, and, if yours has a trademark or copyright, do you defend your brand, including cease and desist letters?

In a year when wearing a mask is mandatory, aviator glasses are hip, and blue jeans is the American uniform, the January 6 criminal defendants looked more like a mail-order catalogue than activists. Unscientifically stated, to my eyes, while it was live streaming, it appeared over 90% of persons on the immediate Capitol grounds and inside the Capitol wore branded clothing, including t-shirts, patches, and hats. The FBI saw the same thing I did and they are capitalizing on it in their identification of defendants. Anything a person wears in public is admissible, and DOJ attorneys are using outfits and gear to create the misimpression that the events of January 6 were committed by sophisticated operatives, instead of a bunch of people who used their credit cards.

As with telling you in the last section that there's a pre-existing allegation that the Oath Keepers membership list is out to a reporter, let me tell you now which piece of clothing to which I award the "fashion *faux pas*" of the day. A patch. Worn by one of the "Oath Keepers" defendants that reads "I don't believe in anything. I came for the violence." It took me one Google search to land on a website from whence it may have been purchased. *At least it's not put out by Oath Keepers* was my first thought. My second was to contact the company to inform them that the patch was being used in legal proceedings and perhaps they would discontinue its production. That was, until I found under the company Q&A "What if I find some of your merchandise offensive?" with an answer "Suck it up, buttercup."

You need to seriously ask yourself whether you want your organization associated with not only people who are not members but who are adorned in pro-violence merchandise that's readily available on the Internet. If you seriously want to protect the Second Amendment, you have to account for not just "who else," but also "what else," is out there. Anticipate marauders and mercenaries.

Those who need the First Amendment Free Speech Clause to protect their advocacy of other civil rights are getting tripped up by confused messaging from a very small segment of the population. Remember: most of America watched January 6 live and then repeatedly. These are the images getting drilled into the American consciousness, in the same memory space as videos of the Twin Towers falling. While persons wearing such garb may think themselves to be hipsters, the media and Congress are doing a much better job of exploiting the images from January 6 for civil rights repression.

I am not suggesting it is a simple conversation or that one solution will fit all organizations. I am, however, putting out there my belief that strategy sessions to anticipate "domestic terrorism" legislation may mean reconfiguring the revenue stream to straight-out donations from members because the organization offers necessary functions, not because the organization hands out yet another t-shirt you add to the stack in your closet.

As for what you put on when you go outside to mow the lawn? It's up to you whether you iron it first or not. It's a lot of years since Sputnik. Look no further than your own phone for who's watching you now.

## 2 – Candidates & Voting

**E.2.a. Lobbying Elected Officials**

**E.2.b. Campaign Support**

**E.2.c. Advancing Candidates**

I'm not going to belabor these points, but I would recommend the double-down. The important functions a Second Amendment organization lends to the fight are good lobbying techniques, campaign support, advancement of new candidates for elected office, blended with holding elected officials' feet to the proverbial fire. Write up 1-page hand-outs and put them on-line, including the names and work contact information for elected officials in your jurisdiction. For key pieces of legislation, prepare contact sheets to reach politicians at their offices based upon sponsorship or anticipated voting, even if not your immediate representative. Invite politicians to speak to membership, regardless of party affiliation, and extend all professional courtesies. Opposition research is the most important part of my work, not going to gun-raffle dinners. It's about proper legislative advancement and defeat, the right politician in office, and an independent judiciary to whom we present plaintiffs with standing.

### E.2.d. GOTV – "Get Out The Vote!"

I do want to say a word about GOTV. For decades, candidates for office have been furnished with "voter registration rolls." These databases include the most recent contact information and the years the voter went to the polls.

In more sophisticated organizations, like labor unions, leaders review voting rolls to chase after members who fail to vote. I would like to suggest that the time has come for this to happen within the Second Amendment Movement. It's one of the first things I did when I opened my chart on characteristics of the "Oath Keeper" defendants. I looked up whether they were registered to vote or not. To take my remark one step further, to look up whether a member has voted in a given cycle means ensuring that membership is registered to vote and that the registration is active to the current residence of the member.

There was recurrent discussion during the hearings on whether a particular member of the military declined or delayed the request to deploy the WDC National Guard once requested. The butting of heads was whether the response included "don't like the optics," meaning of armed National Guardsmen surrounding the Capitol against American demonstrators (at that point). I mentioned how badly pro-violence hits middle America. What if it could be flipped? Ask yourself this: how can our organizations, collectively, create a visual to show unity and purpose? How do we recover from the public relations disaster of January 6 and how do we push-back against the smear? It has to be with unequivocal patriotism that simultaneously serves the goals of the organization.

For years, I've heard leadership moan about there are XX numbers of gun owners, if only they would vote we would have an easy victory! So: figure it out. Ditch the merchandise that isn't helping, do one good logo, and make members earn it through verifiable methods. Most of us were Boy or Girl Scouts. We're used to earning our badges. Legally incentivize the vote.

I'm running this line of thought not because I have the solution. I'm spending the space on it because strength is going to come through a unified public relations counter-campaign that addresses problems seeping in between the cracks for years before January 6. It has been thirteen years since the *Heller* decision and the activation of the Second Amendment. Hell, the NRA was founded in 1871, and the ACLU in 1920, and at this point – *yes* – they belong in the same sentence.

If you're not going to register to vote, but you carry a cell phone, go register. No more excuses. Leave a true mark on history for freedom, instead of paying your cell phone carrier to ping away the civil rights the rest of us are working to keep.

## 3 – Bill Watch

At least for the balance of 2021, I am asking you to augment your routine bill watch activities with an eye towards the Hill on "domestic terrorism" bills. You're used to tracking Second Amendment legislation. Some organizations, like New York State Conservation Council, publish guides to its members, as well as legislative position memos and statements. Others compile year-over-year bound booklets, so members can see bill origination dates, sponsors, any abrupt change in activity, ranking across bills seen as positive/negative to the organization. Bill tracking happens to be something Second Amendment groups do exceptionally well.

Basis the timing of this White Paper going to press, I have been drawing your attention to two federal bills, mentioned more than once, already:

1. "The Terror Intelligence Improvement Act of 2021"
    - S.183; Sen. Rubio (R), Sponsor
    - [no House Bill]

2. "The Domestic Terrorism Prevention Act of 2021"
    - H.B.350; House Sponsor Rep. Schneider (IL-10, D) + 204 Co-Sponsors
    - S.963; Senate Sponsor Sen. Durbin (IL, D) + 2 Co-Sponsors

At Appendix 1 and Appendix 2, you will find tear-out opposition letters to the Bills. These letters are meant for you to fill in the missing two Senators of the state in which you reside (and, hopefully, are registered to vote). You can find the Senators' names and mailing addresses at www.Senate.gov. Make the indicated number of photocopies, sign each as an original, and mail them off by first class mail.

What is it that I did to create these 1-page opposition letters? I used a repeatable structure that I'll lay out here for you, so that you can replicate it for other legislation where you are pro/con. What I've found through decades of activism is that giving membership an activity that can be executed in ten minutes or less on an issue that is clearly related to their personal firearms ownership gets a very high rate of participation.

For purposes of this White Paper, I provide a generic opposition letter. You are, of course, welcomed to write a personal letter. Or both. My logic is generally simple: if the generic letter provided hits the mark, I sign it and get it off. When (and if I remember) I find more time, I write a personal letter. I would rather oppose a caustic piece of legislation more than once than not at all.

When you're ready to write your own 1-page opposition (or support of) letter to a legislator, here's a formula I've found highly successful over the years.

Essential structure of a 1-page activist letter in four paragraphs:

**Paragraph 1**: in one sentence, state your support of or opposition to the piece of legislation by bill number, title, and date.

**Paragraph 2**: in 2-3 sentences, state facts plus sources that support your position. The facts may come from written materials, which you should properly reference, and/or if short enough that you could include for ease of the recipient's reference. The facts may also come from your life experience – a hugely persuasive approach that can also evoke the emotional reaction of the reader.

**Paragraph 3**: in 2 sentences, state your best, recent, and relevant credentials.

**Paragraph 4**: in 1-2 sentences, offer an alternative or state what is already in a law that achieves the same end.

A few remarks to help you navigate this outline.

<u>Paragraph 1</u>: easy enough. And if you don't have the information for a federal bill go to Congress.gov. For any state bill of interest, there will be an equivalent government search engine.

<u>Paragraph 2</u>: facts that support your position. Facts. Not opinion. Position. Not opinion. You might instinctively want to say "no" to every word that limits firearms ownership and use, but that's not going to get you past the secretary and onto the legislator's desk. Why? They've heard all the opinions already. All the snark and the raised voices and name-calling. They turn on a deaf ear. Give them something of substance and it will get read.

Second Amendment activists are subject matter experts. We attend a considerable number of meetings per year at which we get tutorials from lawyers and judges and District Attorneys and other members. Heard something but can't quite remember it? Pick up the phone. Speakers want to be contacted weeks later by someone who was impressed enough by their presentation to bother to contact them for clarification or citation. Especially if you are writing to a peer-level legislator (e.g., a county legislator concerning a point made by a district attorney), your reference to a talk given by a colleague may well drive the legislator to reach out to that peer for further discussion. You should also not hesitate to offer your availability to a legislator, if your education, training, career, or leadership role makes you a resource to get a legislator through the weeds of a particular bill.

The single biggest mistake you can make when speaking to or writing to a legislator is to hoist upon them the requirement that they "should know." No. completely flip your attitude. No one knows everything. And the further a bill drills down into minutiae, the less likely it is that the legislator understands it. By offering a tapas of solid information, your letter gets past the secretary, might even be used to look up those sources by the legislative aide, and will get noticed and retained by the legislator. It could possibly even be passed forward from the legislator to the sponsor with a "Did you see this?"

If you are looking at opposition to a complex bill, covering more than three specific action items, pick one. You can always write another letter, the following week even, about another point in the bill. But don't allow yourself to get slowed down and don't bog the legislator down, with too much detail in that 1-page (two if absolutely necessary) letter. Get your opposition in front of the legislator; be counted; and then get out.

The exception to this is to write an entirely different form of opposition, in the manner of a short White Paper, a briefing memo, or a cover letter to an already published piece with your authorship credit. Or, the other exception, if your 1-page letter is sufficiently catchy, you may be called by staff or the legislator to ask to submit something further – and you will want to do so.

Paragraph 3. Your best credentials – meaning what others say when they introduce you. In my case: an attorney. It's not what I would say is how I introduce myself because it carries too much connotation as a profession in general population settings. But, it is the credibility card. 'I am an attorney writing to comment on proposed legislation' will get that letter further up the political chain than 'I am writing to comment on proposed legislation as an award-winning writer of short stories'…unless it is about funding for the arts. (You get my point.)

Your recent credentials – meaning immediate past, not life's biography, unless it was a life-changing experience like surviving a plane crash or an objectively-high accomplishment like the 1964 Olympics or a universal experience of positive emotional connotation like when I was just a kid Michael Jordan leaned over and said, "You wanna see who can jump higher," with a twinkle in his eye. It's not a job interview or a one-up contest. You are simply demonstrating a recent connection to the issue at hand, so as to be perceived to be relevant in your remarks.

Your relevant credentials. This one is a little bit trickier. It may be that what causes you to oppose a bill is because you enjoyed hunting as a kid with your father and grandfather and now you want to pass that experience on to your grandchildren. That's relevant. And it spans your life's journey. Perhaps you once won a medal in a shooting competition as a kid and now are a coach of a youth shooting travel team. Again, life's journey, tugs at heart strings, completely relevant. Look for the reason the legislator should want to believe you and credit you for what you have learned along the way.

Four more points about the four-paragraph activist letter, and then I'll move on.

Tone. If you can't be professional and leave the curse words and opponent slams and legislator insults off the page, then don't do it. You're wasting your time, paper, ink, and postage. It does not matter how gnarly the legislator is him or herself. It doesn't matter their political party. It doesn't matter their age or whether they brushed their hair that morning or not. Be professional. Write a letter you can photocopy and pass around the gun club and ask others to use as a template for their own letters. Write a letter you can send to your local newspaper as an "open letter to legislators" and ask the editor to publish. We are on a public relations campaign.

Colored paper. When I'm doing a run of activist activities, especially if it's during a run of speaking engagements at different organizations, I use different colored papers. Camo orange. Lime green. Canary yellow. Bright pink. Helps me to keep things straight as I grab my materials to go to a meeting, for one. It also helps a group send a message that there is more than one of "me" out there, noticing a bill, making the effort to voice a position, and expecting a response. Believe it or not, it also helps members of multiple groups to know if they already did the letter at another meeting.

Postage. When you engage at a group meeting: take envelopes, labels, and stamps. Literally offer folks to do the complete through to licking the envelope closed and you then deliver them to the post office. We're all busy. Don't let a captive audience leave you without the opportunity to make it happen. Then, when people offer to make donations or they pass around the hat, they know what it's being used for beyond your gas. Increase the donations through showing a specific purpose.

Follow-up. If you do this right, you're going to have contact from folks with questions. Even as I draft this book with not one, not two, but three calls to action, I am asking myself why I am self-inflicting the level of feedback I'm expecting. Those e-mails, voicemails, and texts, and even photocopies mailed to you of folks' letters is part of sharing the experiencing, so be prepared to answer questions. Every single question teaches you what to do better next time to make it (a.) easier for people to engage as an activist in support of the Second Amendment; and, (b.) more likely to bring others to the table. Almost every gun club, informal, and certainly formal organization has a website – this, too, can be space for a transparent call to action. There is nothing to hide about increasingly sophisticated activism that directly correlates to the legislative process. I chose letters because it's an easy one to incorporate into an already lengthy White Paper. Another day, we'll need our own *Politics the Wellstone Way*.[373] For now, read that one. (You'll also find it on Amazon, LOL.) Phone banks. Lobbying days. Individual legislator meetings. Even bill drafts. If it's not in your wheelhouse, it needs to be, and soon. We're going to have one shot at pushing back against "domestic terrorism" legislation. Make it count.

## 4 – Legal Defense Funds

While I am of the belief that, in general, the defendants of January 6 events who are making headlines are not Second Amendment supporters, it forces the issue of lawyers and the Second Amendment, funding for civil rights litigation, and coalition building.

Allow me to dispel any preconception that Second Amendment lawyers are as plentiful as DWI attorneys or personal injury lawyers. There are so few attorneys with a practice dedicated to Second Amendment issues that you can basically meet them by attending one year of NRA and Second Amendment Foundation conferences. It is a literal impossibility to file lawsuits against every unconstitutional law infringing or potentially infringing the Second Amendment because there is a critical deficit of Second Amendment lawyers.

In your locale, you may have one or more attorney competent to handle, e.g., pistol permit matters, but is he or she admitted to each of three levels of federal courts, if needed? And, given how precious few Second Amendment cases have been accepted by the United States Supreme

---

[373] WellstoneAction!, Politics the Wellstone Way: How to Elect Progressive Candidates and Win on Issues (University of Minnesota Press, 2005) at https://www.upress.umn.edu/book-division/books/politics-the-wellstone-way

Court since 2008, your odds of hiring an attorney who is properly licensed, competent, and has appeared before the Court is less than about ten (10), total, out of 1.3 million attorneys nationwide.[374]

It takes years to become an experienced attorney. It costs money to run an office. And, it is a job. It's unrealistic to expect attorneys in private practice to handle firearms cases *pro bono,* to say nothing of the magnitude of work that goes into pure federal civil rights litigation.

And yet: it remains shocking to me, near fifteen years into this practice area, how many calls I get asking for my representation, for free, even by people working and earning a good living.

This is a tension as old as the Constitution. Having read widely about the struggle for civil rights since 1905 and having spoken with other attorneys, including attorneys in other civil rights practice topics, the tension is real. You think a law is unconstitutional and unjust and you shouldn't have to fight it, so don't want to pay me or any other lawyer. You lump us into the corral of the bad guys. We are on your side. This is an occupation and a calling. And a license, to say nothing of a Code of Professional Responsibility. To say nothing of the "zealous representation" schtick.

When I look to successful models, I look to the NAACP, the ACLU, Amnesty International, Electronic Frontier Foundation, the Socialist Workers Party of America, the United Farm Workers, and other unions. What these organizations have in common is their commitment to developing in-house counsel or having private counsel on retainer in long-term relationships.

The leading reason for such an approach is money. To bring an attorney in on salary is much cheaper than hiring an attorney on an hourly basis. It also allows you to attract and retain talent, to build files that become the intellectual property of the organization, and to boost your fundraising for legal services. Also, the organization picks up coverage for additional issues, like By-Laws, membership criteria, and litigation witness or document production requests.

That's what I would call the "gold standard."

On a smaller scale, I would suggest it is time for more *amicus curiae* briefs, meaning "friend of the court." An organization(s) – or even an individual person(s) – can submit a brief to a federal court at various stages of lawsuits. The *amicus curiae* brief offers the court supplemental

---

[374] "ABA Profile of the Legal Profession: 2020," American Bar Association (July 2020), p. 2 at https://www.americanbar.org/news/reporter_resources/profile-of-profession/

expertise, particularly in cases involving watershed issues. It also lends fresh eyes to lawsuit documents into the thousands of pages. It adds variation in the voices and perspectives. And it offers more sources for judges to plagiarize when writing their decisions.

It is also affordable. The *amicus* brief is cheaper because it's a single document with a word limit, such that one could, for example, negotiate a "not to exceed" rate with an attorney. Cheaper because more than one group or person can join the *amicus*. In one *amicus* brief I submitted, we gathered more than 150 groups and individuals, asking $100/each of them. The brief was also a victory in that every organization/person making a financial contribution was required by court rule to be listed and described at the front the brief. Ours looked and read like a grassroots petition to the Court. It was a historic, novel use of a standard form in square compliance with the rules.

As a bottom line on the subject, what I am saying is that it's time for organizations to design and implement some form of financial participation in the legal flank of the Second Amendment Movement. Perhaps that will mean the organization votes to contribute $250-$1,000 towards the legal defense funds of a member defending his or her permit, and, as part of that process, the lawyer is invited to speak to the organization, generally, and in a non-identifying matter, about concealed carry law in your area. Hopefully, it means that your organization will authorize an outreach to larger groups within the state or country to ask, "How can we help?" The answer may be a financial contribution with acknowledgement in the next publication to boost good will. It may be joining as a co-amici.

The inverse of what I am saying about lawyers at the top is true about the bottom of the judicial pyramid. There are lawyers and there are many cases that are the bread-and-butter of the Second Amendment happening every day of the week, particularly at the county court level. Those cases, which are more likely to involve your membership can sustain and slowly build upon the foundation of our Second Amendment rights. Not every case will or needs to be a SCOTUS contender, but all aspects of our civil rights must be defended at this point.

## 5 – Go Back (To a Simpler Way of Doing Things)

The Electronics Age needs to be brought to an end. Ditch the cell phone. Stop taking "selfies" and other photos you never print. Kill the social media accounts where you are writing scads of regrettable things. Buy a radio, a film camera, a landline, and an attached answering machine.  Send your mother a greeting card through the United States Postal Service.  You can still buy Bic blue ink ballpoint pens.

You have paid Zuckerberg, Bezos, and other billionaires – *billions,* literally – to usurp your civil rights.  Every time you use modern electronics, you waive your rights of privacy.  Old caselaw is good caselaw for "old" technology.  You're the one giving away your rights.  At least make them work for a warrant and knock at your front door.

Again: I'm not talking about breaking the law.  This is about rebuilding civil rights to strengthen our First Amendment rights to free speech and assembly, our privacy rights, our Due Process rights, our Equal Protection rights, as Second Amendment supporters and activists.  It's cliché among judges: "expectation."  You restore privacy and speech and assembly and the entire apparatus of government interaction with you when you respect yourself.

---

"The NSA targets the communications of everyone. It ingests them by default. It collects them in its system and it filters them and it analyzes them and it measures them and it stores them for periods of time, simply because that's the easiest, most efficient, and valuable way to achieve these ends. So while they may be intending to target someone associated with a foreign government or someone that they suspect of terrorism, they're collecting your communications to do so."

Edward Snowden, 2013
The Hong Kong interviews by The Guardian

---

Most critical activism work is done at the local and county levels.  Of late, it's where numerous inappropriate and unconstitutional gun bills are numbered and passed.  Start walking around your neighborhood.  Make personal telephone calls on landlines, have in-person meetings, and send handwritten letters in No. 10 envelopes – these are the kinds of activities that effectively blocks those bills.  It's also easier, cheaper, and faster than suing afterwards.

I'm calling for national-level activism.  Look at how I'm doing it: a book for sale with letter templates for you to sign and send to Washington, D.C. and a recent copy of the U.S. Senate telephone directory.  I'm being transparent.  This is constitutionally-protected activism.  And, it spreads as soon as you add your name to the template letters in Appendices 1, 2, and 4 and drop them in the mail, then pick-up that telephone receiver for the follow-up call.

This is where, sadly, those who entered the Capitol on January 6 were mistaken. Their actions were too little and too late, if the objective was to keep President Trump in the White House. No matter how or when they went about a physical attack on the Capitol building or even if Members of Congress had been killed, the American people would not have tolerated an attempted violent overthrow of the United States government. It was disproportionate to the current circumstances.

Which is why my first thought was "What the hell is going on here?" and then "*Shit!* What's in the legislative hopper?" When all else is political chaos, stand still and look quietly moving only your eyes. You'll see through the smoke and mirrors. You'll also see who else isn't running. Look them straight in the eyes. We are The People.

You think January 6 is the first time something like this has happened? Go Google the "RNC 8 2008" and "21 Panthers 1974." Read *Schenck v. U.S.*, 249 U.S. 47 (1919), *Abrams v. United States,* 250 U.S. 616 (1919), *Frohwerk v. U.S.,* 250 U.S. 616 (1919), and *Debs v. U.S.,* 249 U.S. 211 (1919) – all prosecuted under the Espionage Act of 1917. We defenders of the Second Amendment have only been at this since *Heller.* The other side of the aisle has been at this more than 100 years.

Welcome to the club.

*Julian Assange*
*The ByLine interviews*
*2015*

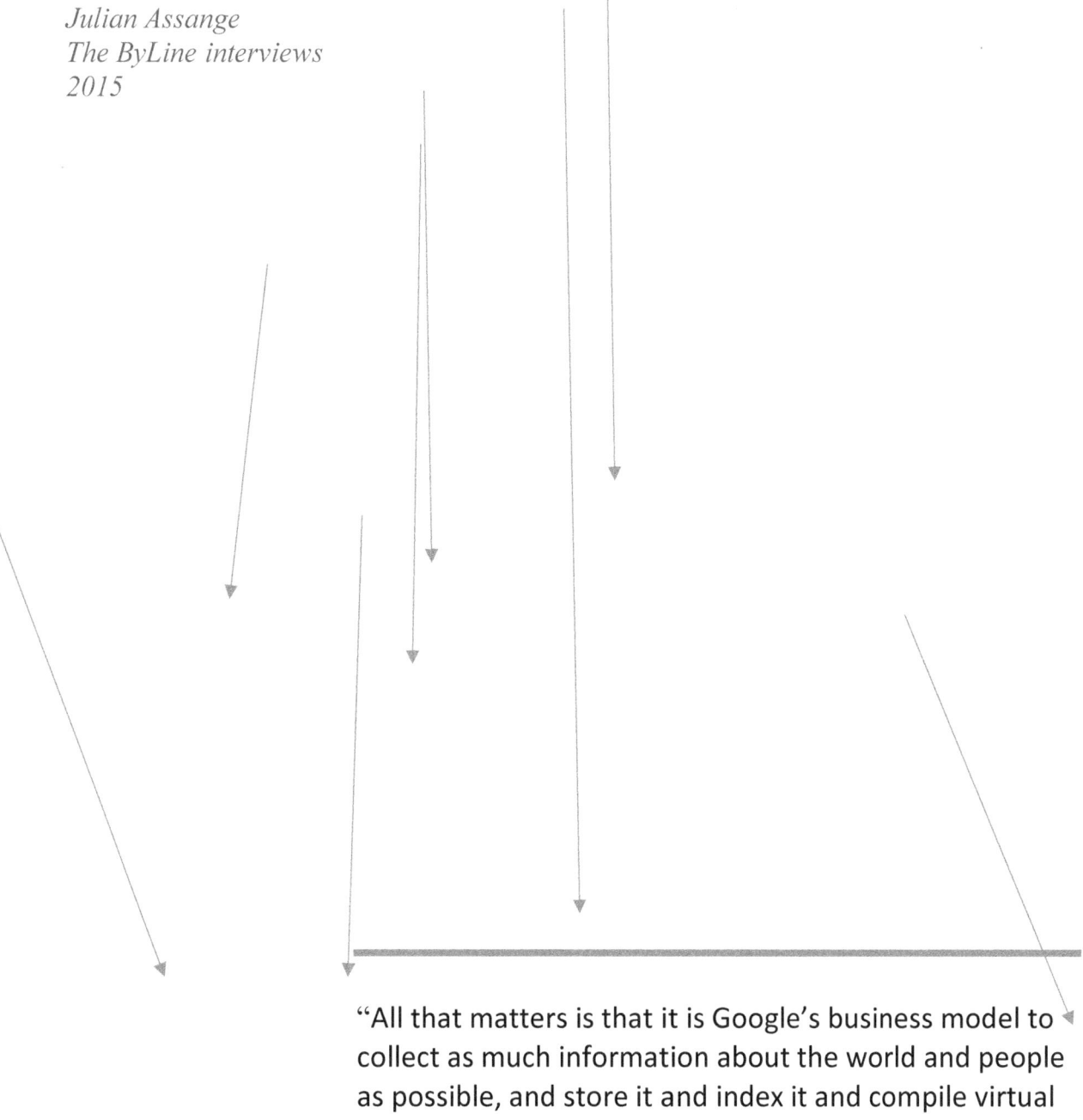

"All that matters is that it is Google's business model to collect as much information about the world and people as possible, and store it and index it and compile virtual dossiers on everyone and predict their behaviour, and sell it to various organisations and advertisers and so on. For any organisation that does that and is based in the United States the US National Security Agency and other intelligence agencies will make sure that they get hold of that information. It's simply too easy to do so and too attractive. It is very valuable information and that gives the US deep state an edge."

# Index

## 1

18 U.S.C. §1361 ................................................ 9
18 U.S.C. §1362 ................................................ 9
18 U.S.C. §1512(c)(1) ........................................ 9
18 U.S.C. §1512(c)(2) ........................................ 9
18 U.S.C. §1519 .............................................. 10
18 U.S.C. §1752(a)(1) ...................................... 10
18 U.S.C. §2 ...................................................... 9
18 U.S.C. §2331 ............................. 49-50, 53, 90, 91
18 U.S.C. §2331(5) ........................... 53[238], *91-92*
18 U.S.C. §2332(b)(g)(5)(B) ........................... 10
18 U.S.C. §2332b(g)(5) ................................... 10
18 U.S.C. §371 ............................................. 9-10
18 U.S.C. §372 ................................................ 9
18 U.S.C. §922(g) ..................................... 49, 68
18 U.S.C. §922(g)(1)-(9) ................................. 67

## 2

28 C.F.R. §0.85 .............................................. 57

## 3

IIIer ................................... 31, *42-43*, 66

## 4

40 U.S.C. §5104(2) ........................................ 15
4chan.com (*see also* Chris Poole) .............. 43, 43 (text box)

## 5

50 U.S.C. §1881a .......................................... 66
50 U.S.C. §1881a(d)(1)(A)-(B) ...................... 67

## 6

6 U.S.C. §101 ................................................ 54
6 U.S.C. §101(16) .......................................... 54
60 Minutes ........................................... 2, 65[282]

## 8

8 U.S.C. §1182(a)(3)(B)(ii) ............................ 54
8 U.S.C. §1182(a)(3)(B)(iii) ...................... 54-55
8 U.S.C. §1189 ......................................... 59[257]
8 U.S.C. §1189(a)(2)(B) ............................ 61[260]
8 U.S.C. §1189(a)(3)(B) ............................ 61[261]
8 U.S.C. §1189(c)(1) ................................. 61[261]
8 U.S.C. §1189(c)(2) ................................. 61[261]
8chan.com ...................................................... 43

## 9

9/11 ............................................. 40, 41, 44-45, 47, 52, 56, 58, 58 (text box), 66, 74, 75, 78, 79, 84, 94

## A

Abrams v. U.S. ............................................. 110
Abu Ghraib prison ......................................... 40
Abu Sayyaf Group ........................... 72 (text box)
Abu Zubaydah ............................................... 79
Accor Augmented Hospitality Hotels ............. 73
"Act Related to Habeas Corpus and Regulating Judicial Proceedings in Certain Cases," 12 Stat. 755 (1863) ........................................... 65[281]
Air Force. *See under* U.S. Air Force.
al'Aulaqi (Nasser) v. Obama ........................ 52
*al'Quaeda* .................. 42, 46, 47, 48, 49, 58, 71

Al-Shabaab .................................................... 47
Alamo Rental Car ..................................... 73[303]
Amazon ...................................... 28, 64, 73, 106
    Bezos, Jeff. ............................................ 109
American Civil Liberties Union ("ACLU")
    .............................. 61 (text box), 66, 101, 107
amicus curiae .......................................... 107, 108
Amnesty International ................................... 107
Amnesty Int'l. (Clapper v.) ............................... 67
Anarchist ........................................ 2, 25, 31, 43
Anarchist Cookbook .................................. 20, 28
Anti-Defamation League ................................ 65
Antifa .............................................. 34, 36, 46
Apple ......................................................... 73[302]
Army. *See under* U.S. Army.
Assange, Julian ........................... 110 (next page)
"Assault Weapons Ban Reauthorization Act
    of 2003" .................................................. 65[282]
AT&T .......................................................... 73[302]
Aum Shinrikyo ............................... 72 (text box)
Austin, U.S. Sec. Def. Lloyd .................... 86, 88
"Authorization for Use of Military Force"
    (2001-2002) (also S.J.Res.23) ................. 51[231]

## B

Babbitt, Ashli ............................. preface, 30, 47
Bacon, U.S. Rep. Don ............................... 73[307]
Bank of America ......................... 63[272], 73, 73[304]
Barrett, Hon. Amy Coney ...................... preface
Basque Fatherland and Liberty ....... 72 (text box)
Best Western Hotels ................................. 73[303]
Bezos, Jeff. *See under* Amazon.
Biden, U.S. Pres. Joseph ............................... 56
Blair, U.K. (former) P.M. Tony ..................... 81

Blanton, Brett ........................................... 32, 35
Blinken, Sec. State Anthony. *See under* U.S. Dep't.
    State.
Blodgett, Timothy .................................... 32, 35
Boko Haram ............................................. 47, 55
Boogaloo Bois (also "boogaloo," #boogaloo)..31
    38 (Donohue paper), 42, 43, 43 (text box)
Brady Act ........................................... 67[287], 68
Budget Group ........................................... 73[303]
    Avis Car Rental ................................... 73[303]
    Budget Car Rental ............................... 73[303]
Bush, U.S. Pres. (former) George W ............. 51,
    51 (text box), 65[281]
Presidential Directive 6 (2004) ................ 67[287]
Bush, U.S. Pres. George H.W. ...................... 50
By-laws ...................................... 95, 97, 98, 107

## C

Calderon v. Clearview AI ............... 80 (text box)
Caldwell, Sharon ................................... 16, 16[71]
**Caldwell, Thomas** ................. *3-4* (membership
    allegations), 7, 9 (charges against), 10 (pre-trial
    status), *15-18* (background), 18[77], 19, 20, *26-28*,
    27 (medical conditions), 88 (military service)
*Caldwell (U.S. v.)* ................................ passim
Carlos, John .................................... 19 (text box)
Carlson, Tucker ...................................... 94, 109
CDW Government LLC ................. 80 (text box)
"Case Study on the Militia-Sphere" (*see also*
    John K. Donohue) ...................................... 37
Cheney, Richard ("Dick") ............... 51 (text box)
Choice Hotels ............................................ 73[303]
Clapper v. Amnesty Int'l. USA ...................... 67
Clearview AI ......................... 80, 80 (text boxes)

# Index

Cognos .............................................................. 18
COINTELPRO ......................................... 43, 66
Communist Party USA (also "Communist,"
 generally) ............................................... 43, 66
conspiracy (*see also* 18 USC §§371, 372)..... 15,
 16, 17, 18, 19, 30, 32, 43, 45, 57
Contee, Chief Robert. *See under* Washington, D.C.
 Metropolitan Police Department.
Cornyn, U.S. Sen. John.......................... epigraph
**Crowl, Donovan** ......................4-5 (membership
 allegations), 5[19], 7, 8, 9 (charges against),
 11 (pre-trial status), 15, 16, 20, 22 (background),
 26 (admissions), 88 (military service)
*Crowl (U.S. v.)* .............................................5[20]
*Crowl (U.S. v. Caldwell, Crowl, et al.)*..*passim*
Cruz, U.S. Sen. "Ted"........................ preface, 87
CyVision Technologies ................................... 37
 Donohue, Jack. *See also.*
 Goldenberg, Paul.................................. 39[193]

## D

Debs v. U.S. .................................................. 110
"Denying Firearms and Explosives to Dangerous
 Terrorists Act" (S.551) (2007-2015)....... 67[286]
de-risking ........................................................ 63
destructive device .....................................20[89], 85
detainee ........................................... *78-79*, 78[321]
 *See also* enemy combatant.
 *See also* "Enhanced Interrogation Techniques."
 *See also* Guantanamo Bay detention camp.
 *See also* U.S. CIA.
domestic terrorist. *See under* terrorist.
"Domestic Terrorism Prevention Act of 2021"
 (also HB350/SB963) ........ 74, 102, App. 1&2,
 App. 3
Donohue, John K. *See under* U.S. Capitol Police.
drone ................................................. *40- 41*, 52
Duckworth, U.S. Sen. Tammy ........................74
Due Process Clause .................. 59, 61 (text box),
 67, 71, 77(text box), 93, 94, 109
DUNS number ...................................... 18, 18[80]
Durbin, U.S. Sen. Richard..............................45,
 74, 102, App. 1&2, App. 3

## E

Eisenhart, Lisa......................................76[310, 311]
Electronic Frontier Foundation ("EFF") ........107
*Elhady v. TSC*................................ 69 (text box)
Elliott, Farar ............................................32, 35
encrypted ..............................................15, 83, 85
 non-encrypted .............................................85
enemy combatant ...........................................41
 *See also* detainee.
 *See also* Guantanamo Bay detention camp.
 *See also* U.S. CIA.
Enhanced Interrogation Tech. (EITs)..............40,
 52, 78-79
Enterprise Rental Car ..................................73[303]
Equal Protection Clause .....................93, 94, 109
exculpatory materials ...........................79, 81, 84
Expedia Group .........................................73[303]
explosive(s) ..................................14, 40, 55, 90
Extended Stay America..............................73[303]
extremism......................................57 (defined),
 57 (FBI terminology), 86 (DOD Working
 Group), 88 (DOD stand-down)

## F

Facebook .................................................... 5,
16, 22, 24, 26, 27, 73[302], 79, 80 (text box), 81,
83, 83[342]

    Zuckerberg, Marc ...................................... 109

facial recognition ................. 82-83, 82 (text box)

Federal Bureau of Investigation. *See under*
    U.S. Federal Bureau of Investigation.

"Federal Courts Administration Act of 1992" .....
    50
    *See also* 18 U.S.C. §2331.

Federal Deposit Insurance Company. *See under*
    U.S. Federal Deposit Insurance Company.

Federal Election Commission. *See under*
    U.S. Federal Election Commission.

Federal Firearms Licensee ("FFL") ........... 62, 66

Feinstein, U.S. Sen. Dianne ........................ 65[282]

firearm ................................................... *passim*

First Amendment ............ 48 (next page), 99, 109

    Assembly Clause ...................................... 143

    Free Speech Clause ............................ 99, 109

FIS Global ....................................................... 62

Fitzpatrick, U.S. Rep. Brian ...................... 74[307]

FlixBus USA ................................................ 73[303]

"Foreign Intelligence Surveillance Act" (1978)
    ("FISA") .................................................. 66

foreign terrorist. *See under* terrorist.

Foreign Terrorist Organization ("FTO") ........ 46,
    52, 57, 59-60, 67, 68, 72, 74

Frohwerk v. U.S. ............................................ 110

## G

Gab AI ....................................................... 73[302]

Gama'a al-Islamiyya ....................... 72 (text box)

Gamma International (U.K.) ........... 82 (text box)

Google ... 43[209], 69, 73[302], 82 (text box), 96, 96[371]

Gorsuch, Hon. Neil ................................. preface

Graham, U.S. Sen. Lindsey ........................ 44-46

Grant, U.S. Pres. Ulysses S. ........................ 65[281]

Grassley, U.S. Sen. Chuck .............................. 50

Greyhound Lines ........................................ 73[303]

Guantanamo Bay detention camp ......... 40, 78-79

    "Report of the Senate Select Committee on
    Intelligence, Committee Study of the Central
    Intelligence Agency Detention and Interrogation
    Program" (2014) .................................... 78-79

    *See also* detainee.

    *See also* enemy combatant.

    *See also* "Enhanced Interrogation Techniques."

    *See also* U.S. Central Intelligence Agency.

Gun Control Act (1968) ................................. 68
    *See also* 18 U.S.C. §922(g).

## H

habeas corpus ............................................. 65[281]

Hal 9000 ................................. 83 (text box), 94

HAMAS ........................................ 72 (text box)

Harrelson, Kenneth ..................... 6 (membership
    allegation, lack of), 7, 9 (charges against),
    12 (pre-trial status), 88 (military service)

    Harrelson (U.S. v. Caldwell, et al.)..*passim*

Hayden, Dir. (former) Gen. Michael. *See under*
    U.S. Central Intelligence Agency.

Heartland Defenders. *See under* militia.

Heller (District of Columbia v.) ...... 93, 101, 110

Hertz Corporation ....................................... 73[303]

Hilton Hotels .............................................. 73[303]

# Index

Hirono, U.S. Sen. Mazie .................... 74
Hizballah (also "Hezballah") .......... 72 (text box)
Homeland Security Act of 2002 ...................... 54
Hyatt Hotels ................................................ 73[303]

## I

Instagram ................................. 80, 80 (text box)
Intercept .......................................... 82 (text box)
Intercontinental Hotels .............................. 73[303]
international terrorist. *See under* terrorist.
Irregulars of Ohio Reserve Militia. *See under* militia.
Irving, Paul .................................................. 33, 35
Islamic State of Iraq and Syria ("ISIS") ... 42, 46, 47, 48, 49, 70, 81

## J

**James, Joshua** ........................... 6 (membership allegation, lack of), 7, 9 (charges against), 12 (pre-trial status)
James (*U.S. v. Caldwell, et al.*) ............. *passim*
Jefferson Lines ......................................... 173[303]
Joint Resolution. *See under* U.S. Senate Joint Resolution 23, "Authorization for Use of Military Force" (2001-2002).

## K

Kahane Chai ................................. 72 (text box)
Kavanaugh, Hon. Brett ............................. preface
kill list. *See under* U.S. President, pre-authorized kill list.
Kirby, Pentagon Press Sec. John. *See under* U.S. Dep't. Def., Pentagon.
Klu Klux Klan ("KKK") ................ 31, 43, 46, 48

Korematsu, Fred Toyosaburo .......................... 65
*Korematsu v. U.S.* .................................. 65[280]
Kroger Company ......................... 63, 63[273], 73[306]
Kurdistan Workers Party ................. 72 (text box)

## L

LaPierre, Wayne. *See under* National Rifle Assn.
labor unions .................................................. 43
Latif v. Sessions ........................................ 66[283]
lethal force ................................................ 74, 92
Liberation Tigers of Tamil Eelam ... 72 (text box)
Lincoln, U.S. Pres. Abraham ...................... 65[281]
LiveLeak.com ................................................. 81
lone actor(s) (*also* "lone wolf") ....................... 70
Lux Bus America ....................................... 73[303]

## M

"Make America Great Again" rallies ............... 34
Maloney, U.S. Rep. Carolyn ...................... 73[303]
Marines. *See under* U.S. Marines.
Marriott International .............................. 73[303]
McInnes, Gavin ....................................... preface
megabus.com ........................................... 73[303]
**Meggs, Connie** ..... 5 (membership allegation), 7, 9 (charges against), 11 (pre-trial status)
Meggs, C. (U.S. v.) ................................... 8[36]
Meggs, C. (U.S. v. Caldwell, et al.) ...... *passim*
**Meggs, Kelly** ..... 5 (membership allegation), 7, 9 (charges against), 11 (pre-trial status), 12
Meggs, K. (U.S. v.) .................... 5[22], 8[36], 96[371]
Meggs, K. (U.S. v. Caldwell, et al.) ...... *passim*
**Mehta, Hon. Amit P.** ... 2, 24, 28[142], 31, 75, 85[348]
membership (defined) ....................... *97-98*, 107
membership (generally) ..... 55, 58, 61, *95-97*, 99

membership (in the Oath Keepers) ............... *4-7,*
   15, 21, 22, 28, 30, 99
Mendoza, Carneysha. *See under* U.S. Captiol
   Police.
Microsoft ....................................................... 16
"Military Comissions Act," 120 Stat. 2600
   (2006) .................................................. 65[281]
militia ................ 4, 13, 16, 17, *20-21,* 28, 29, 30,
   31, 37, 38, 42, *63-64,* 66
   Heartland Defenders .................................... 21
   Irregulars of Ohio Reserve Militia .............. 21
   Ohio State Regular Militia ..................... 4, 20
   Reapers Constitutional Militia .................... 21
Minority Report ......................................... 14, 39
**Minuta, Roberto** ...... 6 (membership allegation),
   7, 8, 8 (text box), 9 (charges against), 12 (pre-
   trial release), 25 (membership/background), 40
   *Minuta (U.S. v.)* .................................... 6[28], 8[34]
   Minuta (U.S. v. Caldwell, et al.) .......... passim
MIT Technology Review ................ 82 (text box)
Mr. & Mrs. America ...................................... 65

# N

National Association for the Advancement of
   Colored People ("NAACP") .................... 107
National Counterterrorism Center. *See under*
   U.S. National Counterterrorism Center.
"National Defense Authorization Act for Fiscal
   Year 2020" .............................................. 55[242]
National Guard (District of Columbia) ........... 33,
   44, 89, 101
   Walker, Maj. Gen. William J., D.C. National
      Guard .................................................... 33
National Liberation Army .............. 72 (text box)

National Rifle Association ("NRA") ......... 41-42,
   42[206], 42[207], 60-61, 72, 94, 101, 106
   LaPierre, Wayne ............................................
   NRA Members' Gun Safety Act of 2013
      (H.R.21) .............................................. 66[286]
National Security Letters ............................... 70
Navy. *See under* U.S. Navy.
Newton, Huey ................. 19 (text box)
News2Share ................................................ 80-81
No-Fly List. *See under* "Terrorist Screening
   Database (TSDB)," U.S. Terrorist Screening
   Center.
non-encrypted .................................................. 80
Norfolk Memo. *See under* U.S. FBI.

# O

Oath Keepers ............................................. *passim*
   *See also* Stewart Rhodes, Founder.
   "Oath Keepers," defined (FBI) .............. *13-14*
   Oath Keepers, Fulton County ..................... 66
   Oath Keepers, Indiana ............................ *63-64*
   Oath Keepers, New York ........................... 66
Ohio State Regular Militia. *See under* militia.
"Operation Choke Point" ........................... *62-63*
Osama bin Laden ................................ 31, 40, 52

# P

Palantir ............................................. 91 (text box)
   Thiel, Peter ................................. 91 (text box)
Palestine Liberation Front ............... 72 (text box)
Palestine Islamic Jihad .................... 72 (text box)
Panther 21 ........................................ 19 (text box)
Paper Chase ................................................... 62
Parker, Bennie Alvin .................. 4 (membership

allegation), 4[13], 6 (membership allegation), 7, 9 (charges against), 12 (pre-trial status)

Parker, B. (U.S. v. Caldwell, et al.) ...... passim

**Parker, Sandra Ruth** ............ 4[13], 6 (membership allegation, lack of), 7, 8[36], 9 (charges against), 12 (pre-trial status)

Parker, S. (U.S. v. Caldwell, et al.) ...... passim

Parler ............................................. 8, 73[302], 80-81

Pasqualini, Atty. Elisabeth. *See under* Ryan Samsel.

Patriot Act (2001) ................................................ 49, 51, 53, 54, 61 (text box), 74

Pentagon. *See under* U.S. Dep't. Def.

Peter Pan Bus Lines .................................... 73[303]

Peterson, Atty. Michelle ................................. 80

pipe bombs ........................................................ 39

Pittman, Yogananda. *See under* U.S. Capitol Police.

Poole, Chris (*see also* 4chan.com) ............... 43[209]

Population Front for the Liberation of Palestine .......................................... 72 (text box)

PFLP, General Command .......... 72 (text box)

Powell, William ............................................. 20[89]

"Preserving Records of Terrorists & Criminals Transactions Act" (S.2935, S.2820) ........ 67[286]

prison ...................................... 10, 24, 27, 50, 74, 75-79 (mistreatment in), 76[311], 85

"Proclamation Suspending Habeas Corpus" (October 17, 1871) ................................. 65[281]

ProPublica ......................................................... 81

Fischer, Ford ............................................. 81

protestor ..................................................... 39, 42

Proud Boys . preface, 2, 23, 31, 34, 42, 43, *45-46*

Proud Boys Canadian Chapter ................. preface

## Q

QAnon (also "Q-Anon" and "Q'Anon") ............... 2, 31, 42, 43 (text box)

## R

Rakoczy, Atty. Kathryn ................ 30 (next page)

Reapers Constitutional Militia. *See under* militia.

Red Coach USA ........................................... 73[303]

Revolutionary Armed Forces of Columbia .......... ................................................. 72 (text box)

Revolutionary People's Liberation . 72 (text box)

Rhodes, Stewart ....... 3, 5[20], 6, 7, 13, 15, 16, 16[69], 19, 25, 25[132], 26, 29-30 (background), 41, 42, 46, 61, 65-66, 87, 96, 98

Robinson v. Sessions ................................. 66-69

Roosevelt, U.S. Pres. Theodore. .................. 65[280]

Presidential Executive Order 9066 (1942) ..................................................... 65[280]

Rove, Karl ....................................... 51 (text box)

Rubio, U.S. Sen. Marco .. 90-92, 102, App. 1&2, App. 3.

## S

SRL Italy ........................................ 82 (text box)

Salesses, Robert .............................................. 33

Samsel, Ryan ....................... 76-77, 77 (text box)

Pasqualini, Atty. Elisabeth .......... 77 (text box)

Sanborn, Jill. *See under* U.S. Federal Bureau of Investigation.

Sandlin, Ronald ............................................... 76

Schaffer, Jon ............................................. *23-25*

Schaffer (U.S. vs.) ....................... 23[107], 24[107]

Schenck v. U.S. ............................................. 110

Schneider, U.S. Rep. Brad ............................ 102, App. 1&2, App. 3

scourge ........................................................... 86

search warrant. *See under* warrant.

Second Amendment ................................ *passim*

Second Amendment Foundation (SAF)...94, 106

Secretary of State. *See under* U.S. Dep't. of State.

Sessions, U.S. Atty. Gen. (former) Jeff. *See under* U.S. Dep't. Justice.

Sherwin, Michael. *See under* U.S. Dep't. of Justice.

Shining Path .................................... 72 (text box)

Siniff, Montana ............................................ 5, 19

Smith, Tommie ................................ 19 (text box)

Specter, U.S. Sen. Arlen ................. 51 (text box)

Signal ................................................ 15, 73[302], 83

Smislova, Melissa. *See under* U.S. Dep't. of Homeland Security.

Snowden, Edward ......................... 109 (text box)

Socialist Workers Part of America (also "Socialists," generally) .................. 43, 66, 107

Southern Poverty Law Center .................... 65, 72

sovereign citizen ...................................... 2, 31, 43

Specter, U.S. Sen. Arlen ................. 51 (text box)

**Steele, Laura** ..... 6 (allegations against), 7, 8[36], 9 (charges against), 11 (pre-trial status), 96, 96[371]

Steele, L. (U.S. v. Caldwell, et al.) ....... *passim*

Stenger, Michael ............................................... 33

Sund, Steven. *See under* U.S. Capitol Police.

surveillance ..................... 1, 67, 76, 82 (text box)

Sutherland Spring Church .............................. 68

Szpindor, Catherine ............................... 32, 35

## T

Taliban ............................................................ 47

Tarrio, Enrique ........................................ preface

"Task Force 1-6, Capitol Security Review" (2021) ........................................................ 34[159]

Telegram ................................................... 73[302]

"Terror Intelligence Improvement Act of 2021" ..................................................... 90, 102

terrorist (also "terrorism") ........................ *passim*

"domestic terrorist" (at law, various) ........... 1, 31, 43, *44-46*, Section C,

"foreign" or "international terrorist" (at law, *see also* 18 U.S.C. §2331) ................. 31, 43, *44-46*, Section B(7),

"Foreign Terrorist Organization" ("FTO") (at law) ..................... 42, 52, 57, 59, 68, 72

"Terrorist Apprehension and Record Retention Act of 2005" (H.R.1225/S.578) ..................... 67[286]

Thiel, Peter. *See under* Palantir.

Thrifty Car Rental ....................................... 73[203]

Thurmond, U.S. Sen. Throm ........................... 50

TikTok ............................................................. 80

T-Mobile ..................................................... 73[302]

Trump, U.S. Pres. (former) Donald .......... preface, 26, 36, 40, 110

Twitter ...................... 73[302], 80, 80 (text box), 81

## U

U.S. **Air Force** ("USAF") ..................... 44, 86[302]

U.S. **Army** .......................................... 18, 20, 88

# Index

U.S. **Bureau of Alcohol, Tobacco, Firearms, and Explosives** ("BATFE" or "ATF") ............... 62, *66-67*, 90
    ATF Form 4473 ........................*66-67*
    National Instant Criminal Background Check System ("NICS") ............... 39, *67-69*, 90

U.S. **Capitol Police** ("USCP") ............... 1, 30, 32, *33-39,* 47, 82 (text box), 89, 92
    "Daily Intelligence Reports" ............... 35
    Donohue memo ............... *36-39*
    Donohue, John K. ("Jack") ............... *36-39*
    USCP, Intelligence and Interagency Coordination Division ............... 36
    Mendoza, Carneysha ............... 32
    Pittman, Acting Chief Yogananda ............... 1, 32, 35, *36-37*, 48, 92 (next page)
    "Special Assessment" (also "the Donohue memo") ............... 36
    Sund, Chief (former) Steven ............... 33, 34, 37, *39-40*
    USCP, Intelligence and Interagency Coordination Division ............... 36

U.S. **Central Intelligence Agency** ("CIA") ............... *78-79*
    CIA black sites ............... 40
    Hayden, Dir. (former) Gen. Michael ............... 79
    See also detainee.
    *See also* enemy combatant.
    *See also* "Enhanced Interrogation Techniques."
    *See also* Guantanamo Bay detention camp.

U.S. **Department of Defense** ("DOD") ............... 60
    Austin, Sec. Defense Lloyd ............... *86-87,* 88
    Pentagon ............... 17, *86-87*, 88
    Salesses, Robert (Assist.) Sec. Def. ............... 33

U.S. **Department of Homeland Security** ("DHS") ............... *32-33*, 34, 39, 74
    DHS, Office of Intelligence & Analysis ............... 35, 55
    "Strategic Framework Countering Terrorism & Targeted Violence" (2019) ............... 58 (text box)
    Smislova, Melissa (Under Sec.) ............... 33, 35
    "Terrorist Threat to the Homeland" (2020) ............... 85 (text box)

U.S. **Department of Justice** ("DOJ") ............... *passim*
    DOJ, Form 361 ............... App. 4
    "Operation Choke Point" ............... *63-64*
    Sessions, Atty. Gen. (former) Jeff ............... *66-69*
    Sherwin, Atty. Michael ............... 2, 14 (text box)

U.S. **Department of State** ............... 60
    Blinken, Sec. Antony ............... 60
    Dep't. State, Bureau of Counterterrorism 59[257]

U.S. **Department of the Treasury** ............... 43, 52, *60-61*, 72, 74
    U.S. Dep't. of the Treasury, Secretary ............... 43, 52, 60-61

U.S. **Federal Bureau of Investigations** ("FBI") ............... *passim*, App. 4
    FBI, Bureau of Counterterrorism ............... 33, 66[283]
    FBI, Collections Operations Group ............... 82 (text box)
    FBI, Criminal Justice Information Services ("CJIS") ............... 39
    FBI, Criminal Justice Information Systems Advisory Policy Board ............... 39
    FBI, "Domestic Investigations and Operations Guide" (2016) ............... 72 (next page)
    FBI, FACE Services Unit ............... 82
    FBI-Norfolk memo ............... 48 (next page),

*36-38*, 45

FBI, Remote Operations Unit..... 82 (text box)

FBI, Terrorist Review and Examination Unit . ............................................... 69 (text box)

FBI, WiFi Group ....................... 82 (text box)

Sanborn, Assist. Dir. Jill.............................1³, 30¹⁴⁸, 33, 35¹⁶⁸, 35¹⁷⁴, 36, 48

"Situation Informational Report" (see also "FBI-Norfolk memo") ........................*36-39*

Wray, Dir. Christopher.............1³, 31, 32, 33, *36-38*, *44-46*, 50, *57-59*, *70-71*, 72

U.S. **Government Accountability Office** ("GAO") ................................................. 34, 34¹⁶⁰, 59

U.S. **House of Representatives**, Committee on Homeland Security, Subcommittee on Intelligence and Counterterrorism (July 16, 2020) (*also under* John K. Donohue)..........38

U.S. **House of Representatives,** House Legislative Branch Subcommittee hearing February 24, 2021 (also by witness)..........................................32

U.S. **House of Representatives,** House Legislative Branch Subcommittee hearing February 25, 2021 (also by witness)..........................................32

U.S. **Internal Revenue Service** ("IRS")............. ................................................... 42²⁰⁷, 64²⁷⁴

IRS Form 990 .............................. 42²⁰⁷, 60, 72

U.S. **Marines** ......................................... 88, 89³⁵⁸

U.S. **Navy** .................................................. 18, 88

U.S. Office of the Inspector General ("OIG") ...................................................................34

OIG, TSC Audit report 07-41..... 69 (text box)

U.S. **President**, pre-authorized kill list......40-41, 52

U.S. Senate Joint Resolution 23, "Authorization for Use of Military Force" (2001-2002)............ 51

U.S. **Senate**, Judiciary Committee, hearing March 2, 2021 (also by witness)................. 33

U.S. **Senate**, Rules and Homeland Security Committees, hearing February 23, 2021 (also by witness).................................................*32-33*

U.S. **Senate**, Rules and Homeland Security Committees, hearing March 3, 2021 (also by witness)......................................................... 33

U.S. **Terrorist Screening Center** ("TSC")........ ....................................*66-67*, 69 (text box), 72

United Farm Workers.................................. 107

Upton, U.S. Rep. Fred .................................74³⁰⁷

# V

Vamoose Bus ..............................................73³⁰³

Verizon Wireless..........................................73³⁰²

Veterans......................... 30, 71, 84, 86-87, 88-89

Violent Gangs and Terrorist Organization File ("VGTOF")...................................... *66-67*, 88

# W

Warner, U.S. Sen. Mark ..............................73³⁰²

warrant.......................................... 1 (number of), 19 (service at Watkin's residence), 70, *82-83*, 96, 98, 109

Washington D.C. Department of Corrections ..... ............................................................. *76-77*

Washington, D.C. Metropolitan Police Department ....................................................24¹¹³, 33, 35

Contee, Acting Chief Robert ................ 33, 35

Index

**Watkins, Jessica**................... *4-6* (membership), 7, 8, 9 (charges), *11-12* (pre-trail status), 13, 15, *19-21* (background), 26, 28-29, 75, 77-79 (prison abuse allegations), 80-84 (exculpatory materials/pre-trial discovery), 88.
    Butler (OH) County jail....................77-78
    Montgomery (OH) County jail.........77-78
    Washington, D.C., Correctional Detention Facility ....................................................... 78

weapon............. 17, 40, 47, 55, 63, 70, 73, 85, 89

white supremacist ............................ 2, 31, 34, 43

Wray, Christopher. *See under* U.S. FBI.

writ of habeas corpus.................51 (text box), 65

Wyndham Hotels ......................................... 73[303]

## Y

**Young, Graydon** .....................5-6 (membership allegations), 7, 9 (charges against), 11 (pre-trial status), 96 (military service)
    Young (U.S. v.)....................... 85[348]
    Steele, L. (U.S. v. Caldwell, et al.)....... passim

## Z

Zello............................................................... 83

Zubaydah, Abu ............................................... 79

Zuckerberg, Marc. *See under* Facebook.

## APPENDIX 1 & 2 – INSTRUCTIONS

Immediately following this instructions page are the three opposition letters for you to complete and mail to specific Senators and Congressmen. The template opposition letters may simply be cut out of this workbook and used or otherwise photocopied.

(1.) Fill in your name/address/the date where indicated.

(2.) Sign on the line where indicated (blue ink is optimal).

(3.) Fill in the names/addresses of your two (2) United States Senators representing your state. There are two (2) for every state. You can locate this information at www.Senate.gov if you are unsure. I recommend using the Washington, D.C. main office address. The second choice would be whichever of the Senators' local offices includes your residence.

(4.) Make three copies of each letter. One is for your records. Mail the other three to the United States Senators on the letter (sponsor + your two).

> - Of course! You may decide to write your own letters. Keep in mind my tips from Section E.3: send the template in the name of getting it done and, when you get a chance, write a personal letter and send it, too. Better two than none.
> - Yes, colored paper. See again Section E.3. You are one person. Together, we become a block. Colored paper helps that point be made.

These same instructions apply to Appendix 1 & 2-B. The House bill version opposition letter found at Appendix 2-A needs only two copies (one for you, one for your Congressman; original to Bill sponsor). You have only one Congressional Representative.

The total number of outbound letters in envelopes is thus:

Appendix 1 = 1 original + 2 copies = 3

Appendix 2-A = 1 original + 1 copy = 2

Appendix 2-B = 1 original + 2 copies = 3

**Outbound Letter Total = 8**

For all of $4.40 in postage, you will have horses in three races. Keep those tickets (letter copies). You'll need them for the telephone follow-up calls in Appendix 3.

Print Your Name:_____

Print Your Address:_____

_____

Date: _____

**U.S. Senator Marco Rubio**
284 Russell Senate Office Building
Washington, D.C. 20510

Dear Senator Rubio:

This letter is written to voice my opposition to **Senate Bill 183, "(The) Terrorism Intelligence Improvement Act of 2021,"** concerning which you are the Sponsor.

Simply stated, I oppose S.183 because:

- it treats the definition of "domestic terrorism" from 18 U.S.C. §2331 as if it is a chargeable crime, which it is not;
- it collapses the definition of "domestic terrorism" into the crime of "international terrorism" and labels it all "terrorism," which risks degrading American activists into being charged as "terrorists;" and,
- no U.S. citizen should be "under a terrorism investigation" by any federal department or agency, especially without notification and all criminal defense rights.

Being "under investigation" – for any crime – is not a disqualifying event from the purchase of a firearm under 18 U.S.C. §922(g). It would violate the Due Process Clause and the Second Amendment. For more than ten, consecutive years, Congress has declined to make being added to the "Terrorist Screening Database" a disqualifying event for precisely the same reason. Due Process matters. The Second Amendment matters.

By copy of this letter to the Senators of my state of residence, I request they decline to co-sponsor S.183 and to join me in opposition to it.

Respectfully,

_____
[sign your name on above line]

**COPY TO:** **U.S. Senator** _____ **U.S. Senator** _____

_____ _____

Washington, D.C. _____ Washington, D.C. _____

APPENDIX-2A: HOUSE VERSION

Print Your Name:_____

Print Your Address:_____

_____

Date: _____

**Congressman Brad Schneider**
300 Cannon House Office Building
Washington, D.C. 20515

Dear Congressman Schneider:

This letter is written to voice my opposition to **House Bill 350, "(The) Domestic Terrorism Prevention Act of 2021,"** concerning which you are the Sponsor.

Simply stated, I oppose House Bill 350 because:

- it treats the definition of "domestic terrorism" from 18 U.S.C. §2331 as if it is a chargeable crime, which it is not;

- it grants future authority to DHS, DOJ, and the FBI to pursue Americans on U.S. soil as "domestic terrorists" in the same manner as Executive Branch intelligence agencies pursue foreign terrorists, even though "domestic terrorism" is <u>not</u> a chargeable crime; and,

- it specifies only one employee per agency will be dedicated to stopping tens of thousands of agency employees from violating the civil rights of Americans, while, at the same time, granting an undefined increase in funding to those agencies to carry out analysis, investigation, and prosecution of "domestic terrorists."

This Bill effectively unleashes the Executive Branch to go after the American people in a manner identical to its pursuit of foreign "enemy combatants" and "detainees." It predictably violates fundamental civil rights, including freedom of speech, assembly, privacy, due process – even basic notice of a crime being alleged.

By copy of this letter to my Congressional Representative, I request s/he decline to co-sponsor H.B. 350 and to join me in opposition to it. If s/he is already a named co-sponsor, I ask my Congressional Representative to withdraw support for the Bill and to vote against it in any Committee vote and any Floor vote.

Respectfully,

_____
[sign your name on above line]


**COPY TO: Congressman** _____

_____

Washington, D.C. _____

Print Your Name:_____

Print Your Address:_____

_____

Date: _____

**Senator Richard Durbin**
711 Hart Senate Building
Washington, D.C. 20510

Dear Senator Durbin:

This letter is written to voice my opposition to **Senate Bill 963, "(The) Domestic Terrorism Prevention Act of 2021,"** concerning which you are the Sponsor.

Simply stated, I oppose Senate Bill 963 because:

- it treats the definition of "domestic terrorism" from 18 U.S.C. §2331 as if it is a chargeable crime, which it is not;

- it grants future authority to DHS, DOJ, and the FBI to pursue Americans on U.S. soil as "domestic terrorists" in the same manner as Executive Branch intelligence agencies pursue foreign terrorists, even though "domestic terrorism" is <u>not</u> a chargeable crime; and,

- it specifies only one employee per agency will be dedicated to stopping tens of thousands of agency employees from violating the civil rights of Americans, while, at the same time, granting an undefined increase in funding to those agencies to carry out analysis, investigation, and prosecution of "domestic terrorists."

This Bill effectively unleashes the Executive Branch to go after the American people in a manner identical to its pursuit of foreign "enemy combatants" and "detainees." It predictably violates fundamental civil rights, including freedom of speech, assembly, privacy, due process – even basic notice of a crime being alleged.

By copy of this letter to my Senators, I request s/he decline to co-sponsor S.B. 963 and to join me in opposition to it. If s/he is already a named co-sponsor, I ask my Senators to withdraw support for the Bill and to vote against it in any Committee vote and any Floor vote.

Respectfully,

_____
[sign your name on above line]

**COPY TO: U.S. Senator** _____ **U.S. Senator** _____

_____   _____

Washington, D.C. _____   Washington, D.C. _____

## APPENDIX 3 – INSTRUCTIONS

Approximately two weeks after you send your opposition letters on the Bills, it's time to place your "be counted" telephone calls. Some of you will excel at writing letters. Some of you – at phone calls. Others would prefer just to stuff envelopes at local political party headquarters or your local gun club. And a few of you will not want to make phone calls. It's difficult to cold call, especially in the current political climate. You expect the worse. You anticipate being hung up on. Or yelled at. Or cut off and stomped.

Me, too. Even after having made thousands of cold calls for politics.

All I can tell you is: write a basic script. Like the opposition letters, the discipline of writing it down will keep you simple. Your goal is to get counted as having phoned-in to oppose a bill. You have to at least spit out your name + bill number + opposition to it. Any/everything else is gravy.

To launch us (yes, I will be doing this, too, as soon as this workbook comes back from the printer), I'm jotting down and sharing with you a basic phone script.

As with the letters, we're all making a total of eight (8) phone calls. Get the list set up first. Fill-in the names and phone numbers on the provided sheet.

Start dialing and keep your notes on the provided sheet.

- Don't let anyone tell you your voice doesn't count unless you call your own Senator. Rubio is the Sponsor. He needs to know.
- If you get voicemail, leave items #1-#3 and state that you will call back. Then: do call back!
- If you get push-back, remember that everyone has bad days. Try taking notes. They won't talk long, if you listen. Then try the pivot "Thank you for sharing that. I've jotted it down. My thoughts are _____ (continue right where you left off – it's the beauty of a numbered script).
- Repeat the same process for your two U.S. Senators.

# APPENDIX 3
## TELEPHONE CALL NUMBERS

### Senate Bill 1834 – the Rubio bill:

Senator Rubio: (202) 224-3041

Your Senator #1 _____: (202) _____-_____

Your Senator #2 _____: (202) _____-_____

### House Bill 350 – the Schneider bill:

Representative Schneider: (202) 225-4835

Your Representative _____: (202) _____-_____

### Senate Bill 963 – the "same as" to House Bill 350

Senator Durbin: (202) 224-2152

Your Senator #1 _____: (202) _____-_____

Your Senator #2 _____: (202) _____-_____

---

The House Telephone Directory is at https://www.house.gov/representatives

The Senate Telephone List is at https://www.senate.gov/senators/senators-contact.htm

# APPENDIX 3
## TELEPHONE CALL NOTES

| Date | Office Called | Bill # | Notes |
|------|---------------|--------|-------|
|      |               |        |       |
|      |               |        |       |
|      |               |        |       |
|      |               |        |       |
|      |               |        |       |
|      |               |        |       |
|      |               |        |       |
|      |               |        |       |
|      |               |        |       |
|      |               |        |       |
|      |               |        |       |
|      |               |        |       |
|      |               |        |       |
|      |               |        |       |
|      |               |        |       |

# APPENDIX 3-1
## S.183 – RUBIO BILL OPPOSITION SCRIPT

1. My name is _____.

2. I'm calling from the state of _____.

3. I am a registered voter and I vote. [If a Republican or Conservative, so state.]

4. I am calling to oppose Senator Rubio's Bill #**183**, "The Terror Intelligence Improvement Act of 2021."

5. My opposition is simple:

   a. the Bill violates the Constitution and the law to investigate Americans as "domestic terrorists;" and,

   b. it infringes the Second Amendment rights of Americans because it doesn't require a criminal conviction to interfere with the right to purchase a firearm.

6. I recently sent a letter to Senator Rubio on _____ (date) in opposition to the Bill. Did you receive it? [If "no," state that you will resend and can fax and e-mail if they will provide that contact information.]

7. Thank you for your time. I appreciate Senator Rubio's actions in many other areas [If you can state something specific, like "U.S.-China trade relations," that's a plus but not necessary]

8. May I ask your name to add to my notes? _____ Thank you, _____ (repeat their name back to them). I look forward to speaking with you, again.

# APPENDIX 3-2
## H.B.350 – SCHNEIDER BILL OPPOSITION SCRIPT

1. My name is _____.

2. I'm calling from the state of _____.

3. I am a registered voter and I vote. [If a Democrat or Working Families Party, so state.]

4. I am calling to oppose Congressman Schneider's Bill #**350**, "The Domestic Terrorism Prevention Act of 2021."

5. My opposition is simple:

   a. the Bill allows the DHS, DOJ, and the FBI to investigate and prosecute Americans as "domestic terrorists" when there is no such crime; and,

   b. it assigns only one (1) employee to stop all the Executive Branch intelligence agencies from infringing the civil rights of Americans in the name of "domestic terrorism."

6. I recently sent a letter to Congressman Schneider on _____ (date) in opposition to the Bill. Did you receive it? [If "no," state that you will resend and can fax and e-mail if they will provide that contact information.]

7. Thank you for your time. I appreciate the Congressman's actions in other areas [If you can state something specific, like "supporting Israel's right to defend herself against Hamas," that's a plus but not necessary]

8. May I ask your name to add to my notes? _____ Thank you, _____. [Repeat their name back to them.] I look forward to speaking with you, again.

# APPENDIX 3-3
## S.B.963 – DURBIN SAME-AS BILL OPPOSITION SCRIPT

1. My name is _____.

2. I'm calling from the state of _____.

3. I am a registered voter and I vote. [If a Democrat or Working Families Party, so state.]

4. I am calling to oppose Congressman Schneider's Bill #**350**, "The Domestic Terrorism Prevention Act of 2021." Senator Durbin is the "same-as" sponsor in the Senate.

5. My opposition is simple:

    c. the Bill allows the DHS, DOJ, and the FBI to investigate and prosecute Americans as "domestic terrorists" when there is no such crime; and,

    d. it assigns only one (1) employee to stop all the Executive Branch intelligence agencies from infringing the civil rights of Americans.

6. I recently sent a letter to Senator Durbin on _____ (date) in opposition to the Bill. Did you receive it? [If "no," state that you will resend and can fax and e-mail if they will provide that contact information.]

7. Thank you for your time. I appreciate the Congressman's actions in other areas [If you can state something specific, like "shaming credit card carriers from raising swipe," that's a plus but not necessary]

8. May I ask your name to add to my notes? _____ Thank you, _____ (repeat their name back to them). I look forward to speaking with you, again.

## Appendix 4 – Instructions

The goal is simple: request a copy of your FBI file, if any.

To do so, you need to submit two pieces of paper to the FBI:
1. a Freedom of Information Act request letter; and,
2. DOJ Form-361, the "Certification of Identity."

The template FOIA letter can be cut out of this workbook, filled-in and submitted with the DOJ Form-361. You can always write your own FOIA letter. Please use only the DOJ Form-361 for its purpose.

Regarding DOJ Form-361, fill in the upper lines for name, citizenship, address, date of birth, and place of birth. It is helpful to include your Social Security Number, although, as per the instructions on this form, it is optional. Skip the "OPTIONAL" section because you are requesting information about yourself. Then sign and date the form.

Make a copy of both the letter and the form for your records.

You may get no response. You may get a standard Bureau letter that says the FBI can neither confirm nor deny. Or you may end up with several pages of paper in your mailbox. If you're particularly special, tens of thousands of pages, as one person I know has received.

Why is the goal to simply request a copy of your file? If nothing is there, your letter is your placeholder to establish a date before which the FBI represents there is no file. Copy in your file; copy in theirs. Given the political "domestic terrorism" freight train, this could prove useful in a worst-case scenario. If it flushes something out, then it is your wake-up call that you are a person of interest against whom future legislation like the Rubio Bill or the No-Fly List could apply.

There is another purpose. To let the FBI know that you are watching them. That we're not afraid to be seen, any more than they should be afraid to be seen by us. Assuming we are law-abiding. Assuming they follow the Constitution.

Let's see how that invitation to have a relationship goes.

Print Your Name:_____

Print Your Address:_____

_____

Telephone (optional): _____

Date: _____

**Federal Bureau of Investigation**
**Record/Information Dissemination Section**
**Attention: FOIA Request**
170 Marcel Drive
Winchester, Virginia 22602-4643

To Whom It May Concern:

This is a request under the Freedom of Information Act.

Date range of request: _____ [year of birth] through present.

Description of request: all records maintained by the FBI in any format, including electronic records, concerning myself.

Full legal name: _____

Any prior name: _____

City/State of Birth: _____

Enclosed is the DOJ Form-361, "Certification of Identity."

I am willing to pay up to $25 for the processing of this request. Please inform me if the estimated fees will exceed this limit before processing my request. No money is enclosed at this time.

I am seeking information for personal use.

Respectfully,

_____

[sign your name on above line]

U.S Department of Justice

# Certification of Identity

FORM APPROVED OMB NO.
1103-0016 EXPIRES 05/31/2020

---

**Privacy Act Statement.** In accordance with 28 CFR Section 16.41(d) personal data sufficient to identify the individuals submitting requests by mail under the Privacy Act of 1974, 5 U.S.C. Section 552a, is required. The purpose of this solicitation is to ensure that the records of individuals who are the subject of U.S. Department of Justice systems of records are not wrongfully disclosed by the Department. Requests will not be processed if this information is not furnished. False information on this form may subject the requester to criminal penalties under 18 U.S.C. Section 1001 and/or 5 U.S.C. Section 552a(i)(3).

Public reporting burden for this collection of information is estimated to average 0.50 hours per response, including the time for reviewing instructions, searching existing data sources, gathering and maintaining the data needed, and completing and reviewing the collection of information. Suggestions for reducing this burden may be submitted to the Office of Information and Regulatory Affairs, Office of Management and Budget, Public Use Reports Project (1103-0016), Washington, DC 20503.

Full Name of Requester [1] _____

Citizenship Status [2] _____ Social Security Number [3] _____

Current Address _____

Date of Birth _____ Place of Birth _____

## OPTIONAL: Authorization to Release Information to Another Person

This form is also to be completed by a requester who is authorizing information relating to himself or herself to be released to another person.

Further, pursuant to 5 U.S.C. Section 552a(b), I authorize the U.S. Department of Justice to release any and all information relating to me to:

_____

### Print or Type Name

I declare under penalty of perjury under the laws of the United States of America that the foregoing is true and correct, and that I am the person named above, and I understand that any falsification of this statement is punishable under the provisions of 18 U.S.C. Section 1001 by a fine of not more than $10,000 or by imprisonment of not more than five years or both, and that requesting or obtaining any record(s) under false pretenses is punishable under the provisions of 5 U.S.C. 552a(i)(3) by a fine of not more than $5,000.

**Signature** [4] _____ Date _____

---

[1] Name of individual who is the subject of the record(s) sought.

[2] Individual submitting a request under the Privacy Act of 1974 must be either "a citizen of the United States or an alien lawfully admitted for permanent residence," pursuant to 5 U.S.C. Section 552a(a)(2). Requests will be processed as Freedom of Information Act requests pursuant to 5 U.S.C. Section 552, rather than Privacy Act requests, for individuals who are not United States citizens or aliens lawfully admitted for permanent residence.

[3] Providing your social security number is voluntary. You are asked to provide your social security number only to facilitate the identification of records relating to you. Without your social security number, the Department may be unable to locate any or all records pertaining to you.

[4] Signature of individual who is the subject of the record sought.

FORM DOJ-361

## 4 AM – Rise & Shine

Can we defeat

– *or at least delay* –

passage of "domestic terrorism"

as a crime

    To preserve rights:

of Free Speech
of Freedom of Assembly
of Due Process
of Privacy
of Equal Protection of the Laws

needed

to defend the Second Amendment?

## 4 AM – Rise & Shine

Can we defeat

*– or at least delay –*

passage of "domestic terrorism"

as a crime

> To preserve rights:

of Free Speech
of Freedom of Assembly
of Due Process
of Privacy
of Equal Protection of the Laws

needed

to defend the Second Amendment?

about the author

*shortest version*

**Paloma A. Capanna,** Attorney & Policy Analyst; Proprietor of Downton Antiques.

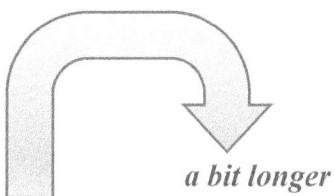
*a bit longer*

**Paloma A. Capanna** is an Attorney & Policy Analyst with more than 25-years of litigation experience, including litigation at the federal and state level for Second Amendment plaintiffs. Notably, **Capanna** represented the plaintiffs in *Robinson v. Session,* which revealed the connection between NICS and the Terrorist Screening Database, and also *McKay v. Cuomo,* which defined 18 U.S.C. §925A as available to individuals seeking to correct an erroneous municipal filing with the FBI of a NICS disqualifying event. Capanna is the recipient of several awards for her work, including the "Defender of the Constitution Award" from WYSL and the Sullivan Policy Institute. **Paloma** currently also holds the nonchalant position of antiques shop owner in North Carolina, which, she points out, "Isn't likely to last much longer, if a Second Amendment activist gets charged with a new crime of domestic terrorism." **She** is a regular guest on radio broadcasts and podcasts, including "The Second Amendment Radio Show" with Bill Robinson on WYSL and "Lock 'N' Load Radio" with Bill Frady. Coverage for this book also includes interviews with AmmoLand News, the Lockwood Phillips show "Viewpoints," radio show host Jim Quinn, and "Assorted Calibers Podcast."

Find out more at 2AMPatriot.com.

www.ingramcontent.com/pod-product-compliance
Lightning Source LLC
Chambersburg PA
CBHW081507080526
44589CB00017B/2675